SAVING OUR CHILDREN FROM POVERTY

SAVING OUR CHILDREN FROM POVERTY

WHAT THE UNITED STATES CAN LEARN FROM FRANCE

Barbara R. Bergmann

Russell Sage Foundation
New York

The Russell Sage Foundation

The Russell Sage Foundation, one of the oldest of America's general purpose foundations, was established in 1907 by Mrs. Margaret Olivia Sage for "the improvement of social and living conditions in the United States." The Foundation seeks to fulfill this mandate by fostering the development and dissemination of knowledge about the country's political, social, and economic problems. While the Foundation endeavors to assure the accuracy and objectivity of each book it publishes, the conclusions and interpretations in Russell Sage Foundation publications are those of the authors and not of the Foundation, its Trustees, or its staff. Publication by Russell Sage, therefore, does not imply Foundation endorsement.

Library of Congress Cataloging-in-Publication Data

Bergmann, Barbara R.
   Saving our children from poverty : what the United States can
learn from France / Barbara R. Bergmann
     p. cm.
   Includes bibliographical references and index.
   ISBN 0-87154-114-9 (cloth : alk. paper)
   1. Child welfare—France. 2. Child welfare—United States. 3. Child welfare—
Government policy—France. 4. Child welfare—Government policy—United States.
I. Title.
   HV268.B47 1996
   362.7'0944—dc20   96-9685
                                                CIP

Text design by Rozlyn Coleman.

RUSSELL SAGE FOUNDATION
112 East 64th Street, New York, New York 10021
10 9 8 7 6 5 4 3 2 1

TO MARY GRAY

✤ CONTENTS ✤

❖ TABLES ❖

✢ ACKNOWLEDGMENTS ✢

FINANCIAL SUPPORT for this study has been provided by the Russell Sage Foundation and the French-American Foundation. The origin of my interest in this field was an invitation from Gail Richardson, now of the Child Care Action Campaign, to participate in a study tour of French child care she was organizing for the French-American Foundation. She has continued to provide encouragement and help, and her energy and sense of priorities have been inspirational to me. Jennifer L. Hochschild, Vee Burke, Nadine Lefaucheur, Gail Richardson, Nancy Folbre, Fred Bergmann, Quentin T. Wodon, Gina Adams, and Arloc Sherman read all or parts of earlier versions of the manuscript and made many helpful suggestions. They are not responsible for any deficiencies in the final version; the remaining errors are my own. Janice Peskin of the Congressional Budget Office has helped to steer me to needed material on U.S. policy. Sherlie S. Svestka and Michele Grgich of the General Accounting Office, as well as Sheila B. Kamerman, Susan Fleck, and Elisabeth Marx were also helpful. Barbara Willer of the National Association for the Education of Young Children and Suzanne Helburn were resources on matters relating to American child-care centers.

During my visits to France, many people were generous with their time and help. I am highly indebted to Christophe Starzec of the Centre d'Étude des Revenus et des Coûts (CERC) in Paris for help and expert guidance, as well as logistic support. Olga Baudelot also was extraordinarily generous in providing information. Professor Edmond Malinvaud was kind enough to intervene with the Institut National de la Statistique et des Études Économiques on my behalf. Thanks are also owed to Betty Duskin of the Organisation for Economic Cooperation and Development, Phillippe Madinier of CERC, Christian Calzada, then of the Social Affairs Ministry, Michel Grignan and Jeanne Fagnani of the Caisse Nationale des

Allocations Familiales, Jacques Zighera of the University of Paris, and Ian Kinn. On the medical side, Dr. Danielle Honegger of the Protection Maternelle et Infantile (PMI) in Lyon and Colette de Saint-Sauveur in Paris provided a great deal of valuable material. Michelle Fillet of the PMI in Paris allowed me to watch some PMI operations. Dr. Marcelle DeLour of the Paris PMI and Dr. Béatrice Blondel of Inserm took the time to point me in the right direction. Nadine Lefaucheur reviewed the manuscript, and her care and expertise were of great help.

Finally, I should like to thank the editors who worked on the manuscript, Alice Tufel and Rozlyn Coleman, whose help is very much appreciated.

Barbara R. Bergmann

✤ PART I ✤

Two Countries, Two Responses

❖ CHAPTER 1 ❖

How Two Countries Respond to Children's Needs

ILLIONS OF CHILDREN in the United States live in deprivation and in circumstances that endanger their well-being
and their chances of becoming reasonably happy, productive, and law-abiding citizens. Many of these children live in
dwellings with broken ceilings and toilets, receive inadequate care,
and have no guaranteed access to medical attention. Many are in
danger of abuse and violence from individuals in their families and
neighborhoods. Many enter the first grade unready for schooling,
set for failure.

In 1993, 23 percent of our children were living below the official
poverty line.[1] Of such children, the bipartisan National Commission on Children has said, "The harshness of [their] lives and their
tenuous hold on tomorrow cannot be countenanced by a wealthy
nation, a caring people, or a prudent society. America's future
depends on these children too."[2] Up to now, however, policy-
makers in the United States have never made a serious effort to
ensure that all of our children get a minimally decent start in life
through governmental action. Neither the New Deal programs of
Franklin Roosevelt nor the Great Society programs of Lyndon
Johnson attempted to do more than palliate child poverty.

There has been widespread realization on both the left and the
right that the current American system of helping poor, single parents and their children, erected in the Roosevelt and Johnson eras,
has not produced a desirable outcome for its clientele or for the

3

country. In the early 1990s, some modest initiatives to change the shape of the system were undertaken. More help was given to parents who were not dependent on welfare and who were struggling in low-paying jobs. Government-supported medical insurance was extended to larger numbers of such families, and a significant increase was voted in the federal payments that supplement those parents' wages. A federal program to help with the costs of child care was also instituted.[3]

At the same time, however, the electorate's animus against single parents who are on welfare and do not work, which had been building since Ronald Reagan's speeches about "welfare queens," continued to grow. Bill Clinton's 1992 campaign for the presidency included a promise to "end welfare as we know it," and in speaking that way—regardless of his intent—he fanned the public's impatience with the welfare system and its clients. Unfortunately, neither President Clinton nor those to the left of him presented an alternative that could be described as a thoroughgoing "reform," one that improved the incentives and abilities of single parents to earn a living and that also promised to reduce deprivation among children.

In 1994, Americans elected a Congress dominated by right-wing Republicans. Their welfare reform program featured a decentralization of the administration of welfare programs, and an end to a guarantee of aid to all eligible families. They proposed large cuts in the funding for public programs that help the families of poor children, both on and off welfare. The main force of their argument is that programs that subsidize unmarried parents create child misery. The way to reduce child misery, they argue, is to discourage teenage and adult behavior that brings infants into the world who are destined to live in poverty by cutting the programs that support them. Whatever the effect of this approach in the longer run, it would be bound in the shorter run to push millions of American children into greater deprivation.

Conservatives in the United States argue that the American system of helping poor, single mothers has been so destructive that "anything" would be better. They believe that the government has little potential for dealing in a positive way with social problems, and that government programs tend to make matters worse rather than better. The experiences of other countries, however, contradict the notion that government programs are inevitably hurtful rather than helpful.

The United States is not the only country with the problem of child poverty. Other high-income nations, particularly those in Western Europe, have wrestled with it. They also have a high and growing incidence of single parenthood; groups within their population suffer from drug and alcohol abuse and from psychological problems. All of these countries have sizable immigrant and minority populations that are marginalized culturally and economically; they have considerable unemployment. These are the kinds of problems that can create large pockets of poverty.

The countries of Western Europe have programs in place that work to shield children and their families from the effects of such problems, as the pioneering work of Sheila B. Kamerman and Alfred J. Kahn has informed us.[4] They have built programs and devoted large sums of taxpayers' money to this effort. On a per capita basis, these countries spend a great deal more money than Americans do for programs benefiting children. They provide income supplements and housing assistance; all of their children have access to medical care under national health insurance schemes; some of these countries provide government-sponsored child care that is free or highly subsidized.[5] The availability of such low-cost child care enables many single parents to take jobs and free themselves from total dependence on government cash grants.

The programs mounted by the countries of Western Europe have achieved a considerable measure of success in insulating children from the grossest forms of deprivation and abuse. In some European countries, as in the United States, 20 to 30 percent of the country's children have parents whose earnings alone could not keep those children from poverty. However, as table 1.1 shows, the European countries follow policies that raise above the poverty line a high proportion of the children who would otherwise be below it. These include programs specially targeted to families with children, as well as programs, like unemployment insurance, that are not but that still help such families. In the United States, by contrast, income-support policies save very few children from poverty.[6] Among the countries listed in table 1.1, the U.S. child poverty rate is by far the highest at 21 percent—way behind the next highest, in Ireland, at 7.6 percent.

TABLE 1.1 HOW TAXES AND BENEFITS LOWER THE PERCENTAGE
OF CHILDREN WHO ARE POOR IN THE UNITED STATES
AND SEVEN EUROPEAN COUNTRIES, 1984–87

	Percentage Poor	
Country	Based on Wage Income Alone	Based on Income After Taxes and Benefits[a]
United States	23.3	21.0
Belgium	21.8	3.6
France	24.7	5.7
Germany	9.7	3.8
Ireland	29.3	7.6
Netherlands	14.3	4.1
Sweden	13.1	3.7
United Kingdom	29.5	7.3

Source: Organisation for Economic Co-operation and Development, "Measurement of Low Incomes and Poverty in a Perspective of International Comparisons," Labor Market and Social Policy Occasional Papers No. 14 (Paris, 1994): 43, table A.6.
Note: The poverty line used in the OECD study is 50 percent of median family income.
[a] Benefits in Europe include children's allowances, housing subsidies, and unemployment insurance. In the United States benefits include unemployment insurance, Aid to Families with Dependent Children (AFDC), food stamps, housing subsidies, and the Earned Income Tax Credit. Taxes include income and social security taxes.

COMPARING FRANCE AND THE UNITED STATES

In the pages that follow, the programs affecting the children of one European country—France—are laid out in considerable detail and compared with our own. The cost of these programs is also presented, to show the size of the financial effort the French have been willing to make. France is worthy of detailed examination because it has adopted a particularly elaborate and generous set of programs designed to enhance and ensure child well-being. In addition to the cash benefits, France has been a leader in providing child care and in setting up a system of preventive medicine for children. Its programs and their efficacy in keeping child poverty low are far less known to the public and to social policy analysts than are those of Sweden.[7] But, like Sweden, France has successfully accomplished a task that we in the United States must eventually tackle.

Differences Between Programs in the United States and France

There is a dramatic difference in expenditure levels between French and American programs that help families with children. When it comes to child care, income supplementation, and medical care, the French spend 59 percent more per capita.[8] The French and American benefit programs are also structured very differently: most of the cash benefits that the American government gives to families with children go to "welfare mothers"—single parents who have no job, and who lose most of their benefits if they take a job. French programs, on the other hand, do not contain this disincentive to work or to maintain a marriage.

French programs send help to a far wider segment of the population than do American programs. Much of the expenditure in France goes into programs that are available to families with children regardless of the parents' income, and regardless of whether there is one parent in the family or two. A large segment of the French spending goes to parents who work at jobs but bring home low wages. Thus, these programs maintain French parents' incentive to get and hold jobs; government help does not desert them when they do so, as is the case in the United States.

One important cultural difference between the United States and France that has an effect on programs that help families with children is the latter's longstanding pronatalism—the response to an historically low birth rate, exacerbated by repeated invasions by neighboring Germany. France's anxieties about the size of its population provided some of the original impetus for programs to provide generous benefits to families with children and have undoubtedly made it easier to rally support for such benefits.[9] French pronatalists had hoped through such programs to coax large numbers of married couples to have big families.

Although these programs have not been successful in achieving that aim,[10] the level of support for them remains high, because another rationale for government support for child well-being is widely appreciated. The French are very proud of their nation and their culture and have a vision of their children as the future bearers of that culture. The country's social programs are perceived as guarding the quality and well-being of France's future adult population, including those who need the most help in becoming productive citizens.[11] These policies have been a great help to families at the bottom of the income scale, particularly single-parent families, although help for the latter was not high on the pronatalists' original agenda.

The lack of a pronatalist agenda in the United States does not mean that these French programs are of no relevance to Americans looking for a new approach to the problems of child poverty. For our purposes, the historical circumstances that led to the adoption of these programs in France are far less relevant than the possibility that variants of them might work well here. If similar programs could raise the living conditions of our poorest children, and improve the incentives for their parents to take jobs and stay together, then such programs deserve to be considered—and the politicians and the public might consider them to be worth their high cost.

Similarities Between France and the United States

While France and the United States differ in many important respects—culturally, socially, historically—their similarities are worth noting. Both are democracies in which citizens enjoy personal freedom and in which most economic functions are carried out by private enterprise. Table 1.2 shows that the two countries have similar rates of growth and rates of investment, despite radically higher taxes in France. France, along with the rest of Europe,

TABLE 1.2 ECONOMIC AND DEMOGRAPHIC DATA FOR THE UNITED STATES AND FRANCE, 1991

Data	United States	France
Population	252,688,000	57,050,000
Per-capita gross domestic product	$22,204	$18,227
Annual rate of growth, 1981–91 (%)	2.2	2.2
Annual rate of investment (%)	2.1	2.3
Taxation as a % of GDP	29.9	43.7
Life expectancy (years)		
Men	72.0	73.0
Women	78.8	81.1
Self-employment as a % of total employment	8.8	8.9
Unemployment rate (%)	6.6	9.3
Women's labor force participation rate, ages 25–54 (%)[a]	72.0	73.5
Births to unmarried women as a % of all births[b]	28	30

Source: Except where indicated, the source is *OECD in Figures,* 1993 edition.

[a] *Contours et caractères; les femmes* (Paris: Institut National de la Statistique et des Études Économiques, 1991), 96.

[b] For the United States, the source is U.S. Bureau of the Census, *Statistical Abstract of the United States, 1993,* (Washington, 1993), 78, table 101; for France, see *La Societé Française: Données sociales, 1993* (Paris: Institut National de la Statistique et des Études Économiques, 1993), 25. The data for both countries refer to 1990.

has considerably higher unemployment rates than the United States does at this time, although in earlier, postwar decades, the rate of French unemployment was considerably lower than in the United States, which suggests that high taxes and benefits are not invariably associated with high unemployment rates. French per capita income is about 82 percent of that in the United States, but life expectancy is somewhat higher. Women participate in paid work to a similar extent in the two countries and the proportion of babies born to unmarried parents is about the same.

In modern industrialized countries the expenses of children's upbringing and the special difficulties of managing a single-parent household are basically the same, whether the country is France, Sweden, or the United States. The cultural and historical differences among countries mean only that such programs cannot be copied from one country to another without extensive adaptation. But the basic structure (as opposed to the details) of a solution to the child poverty problem that works well elsewhere is worth examining by a country such as ours, which has not hit on a satisfactory, home-grown solution. So the types of policies that have worked in France might be useful here if we can find a way to get around the roadblocks that our unique traditions present.

ACTION DIFFICULT BUT NOT IMPOSSIBLE

Timothy M. Smeeding, a leading student of poverty problems in the United States and Europe, showed in a 1992 article why the U.S. system of benefits to families with children does not work well as an anti-poverty system.[12] But it was not really intended as one. Its purpose has been to keep single parents and their children from extreme and scandalous want, from starving and homelessness. It is not designed to achieve their rescue from poverty. There is little discussion in the United States about the desirability of ending child poverty; as a result, the country has not yet even aspired to such a goal, much less started to formulate a policy to achieve it.

It is easy to identify a set of reasons that explain why progress in alleviating child poverty has been so difficult in the United States. They include the anti-tax and anti-government strain in our national character that has become an increasing part of our political discourse, based in part on perceptions that the government has not performed well in many areas and that money devoted to government is largely wasted. Our ideology of individualism holds that people ought to stand on their own feet and that government help undermines the habit of independence. Many unattractive behaviors are attributed to the parents who are the direct beneficiaries of government benefits for children—an avoidance of work, disorderly family relations, loose sexual behavior, the feckless procreation of children the public must support, and the misspending of the money they receive for necessities on "luxuries" and "vices."

The anger against poor children's parents is in part connected to the problem of race relations in the United States. Americans are acutely aware that blacks make up a disproportionately high share of the poor. Some whites (and some blacks as well) incline to the view that those blacks who fail to achieve a middle-class status owe their troubles to innate or learned deficiencies, and their own behavior, rather than to any disadvantages unfairly forced on them by white society. The disproportionate share of crime that is committed by blacks is a further incitement to animus against black people, and certainly contributes to a disinclination to increase the help the government provides to the black community. Most people would not openly say that preschool black children, who are innocent of any delinquency, do not need or deserve more help. But the widespread antagonism against black people undoubtedly contributes to the opposition to giving poor families—widely but falsely perceived to be black—any more help.

Of course, the attitudes that militate against expensive and elaborate programs to help children are by no means unknown in the countries of Western Europe, France included. It is sometimes said that the European countries have been able to achieve low child-poverty rates because of their "homogeneous populations," perhaps a euphemistic way of saying that they do not have the racial problems that we do. While differences in skin color are less of an issue in Europe than in the United States, parts of the European population harbor considerable resentment against people who are distinguishable by ethnicity, religion, or origin from the majority. In Europe, as well as in the United States, there is disgust at the rise in single parenthood, impatience with a high burden of taxation, exasperation at flaws in the government-run medical insurance system, and worry that too much government spending and government activism hurts economic growth. In France and Sweden, left-leaning parties have been defeated and replaced in government by those of a more conservative bent. However, these new governments have done little to water down the structure of benefits for children that were erected by their more leftist predecessors.

The French example shows how timid and modest have been the suggestions of reformers in the United States. It is possible that the very modesty of their proposals, and the small likelihood that their proposals would lead to any great improvement, helped to open the way to the Republican proposals, for which radical results are claimed.

The turn in American politics marked by the Republicans' 1994 capture of the U.S. Congress is, of course, directly opposite to one that would take the American system in the French direction. The lessons we can learn from the French experience will have to be used, if they are used at all, in some future attempt to reform welfare—the one that might follow whatever "reform" the congressional Republicans enact and come after the effects of that "reform" are observed and understood. Perhaps, by then, the American electorate will be ready for a radically different approach—one that is less punitive.

When that time comes, the example of what another country has had the energy and dedication to do for its children should be of interest to Americans. It can serve to promote an eventual understanding of what a considerably more ambitious program to help children can achieve: allow families to live decently, through programs that encourage and enable work, and that help keep families together.

✤ CHAPTER 2 ✤

Differences in Spending and Program Design

THE SIMPLEST WAY to compare the effects of American and French programs on child poverty is to think about a single mother in each of the two countries and about the situation she faces. Assume that both of the mothers have had a couple of children outside of marriage, a common occurrence in both countries as we have seen.

The American mother can go on welfare and stay home with her children, or she can try to support herself and her children by getting a job. If she depends on welfare, she might get benefits worth about $7,500 a year, depending on the state in which she lives, and she will get free health insurance. She and her children will live below the poverty line, probably in a rundown and dangerous neighborhood. However, the family's health-care and child-care needs will be met. The larger society will view her as a failure, as a drain on the honest and industrious taxpayer who has to subsidize her loose morals, as a person of very low standing; she may view herself that way, too.

Her alternative is to get a job. If, like most poor women, she has not had a college-level education, her job will require few or no skills and will be low-paying. A minimum-wage job would pay $8,800 a year, and she would be eligible for government grants worth about $3,400.[1] After taxes, her income would be about $3,900 more than it would have been if she remained on welfare, surely a modest reward for a year of forty-hour weeks of hard work. Moreover, she will have to buy some expensive goods and services she would get for free if she were on welfare. When she leaves welfare for a full-time job, her right to government-paid health insurance lapses, if not immediately, then in a year; her job will probably not carry health insurance benefits. A serious illness will bring an immense financial burden, one that she very likely will be unable to meet. In addition, because she is now working outside the home, she may have to start paying someone else to care for her children. Those single mothers who have to pay for child care use 21 percent of their income, on average, for that purpose.[2]

The American mother's life as a job holder will be much more difficult than her life on welfare, and her standard of living may even be lower. In other words, she and her children are likely to be poor no matter what she does. The low-skilled American mother has little incentive to leave welfare for a job, and that is why all of the "welfare reform" efforts—mostly aimed at training welfare mothers for low-wage jobs—have failed.

The French single mother's alternatives are considerably better. If she has a child under three, she can stay home on a welfare-like program that, in 1991, paid about $8,800 a year, a bit higher than the analogous set of benefits her American counterpart gets. However, if she takes a job, she does far better than her American counterpart. The French minimum wage in 1991 would pay $10,000 to a worker with a full-time year-round job. At that wage, the French single mother is eligible for an additional $6,000 worth of benefits from the government. She does not lose her health insurance if she leaves welfare and takes a job. She will have to pay little or nothing for child care, especially if her children are above age two-and-a-half. Unlike the American mother, then, the French single mother and her children do not have to live in poverty. With a job, she can support them at a decent standard. The French single mother has a far greater incentive to take a job than the American; doing so represents a step up in living standards and quality of life.

The relative advantages of welfare and work in the two countries are reflected in the proportion of single mothers in each country who continue to depend on welfare: despite the far lower standard of living the American welfare benefit provides, a higher proportion of American single mothers remain on welfare. As of December 1991, about 23 percent of French single mothers (and a very small number of single fathers) were receiving welfare-like benefits; most of the rest had jobs or were looking for work.[3] In the United States, 4.7 million of the 7.0 million households headed by a single mother with children, or 67 percent of such households, received welfare payments through Aid to Families with Dependent Children (AFDC).[4] Because of the smaller proportion of single mothers who depend on welfare in France, the total cost of providing the benefit is smaller than in the United States, even though what the family receives is more generous.

Most of the benefits the French single mother gets are available to couples. Some of the important ones—including some cash payments, the free full-time nursery schools for preschool children, and government health insurance—are available to parents in the middle- and upper-income groups. Giving these benefits to every family increases the cost of the French system as compared with the more narrowly targeted American system. But by extending benefits to the job holders and to the married, it does not deter job holding or marriage, as the American system does. Targeting a large group of beneficiaries makes the system politically more popular and probably keeps the quality of the services high.

OVERVIEW OF THE FRENCH AND AMERICAN PROGRAMS

The dozens of French government programs that provide special help for families with children can be grouped under three main headings: child care and development, income supplementation, and medical care. The United States also has programs under each of these headings, serving analogous functions. The differences in French and American programs—in who is entitled to participate and in what is provided—contribute importantly to differences in the extent of child poverty in the two countries.

French child-care programs include public nursery schools, which enroll almost all children between ages three and six, public centers for the care of infants and toddlers, paid maternity leave, and various subsidies for parents' out-of-pocket child-care expenses. In the United States, the analogous (but very different) major programs for preschoolers include Head Start and public kindergarten. The basic difference between the two countries' pro-

grams is that the French spend more and do more. The French provide for "child-minding"—the day-to-day care required when a
parent goes to work—as well as for child development. In the
United States, government programs provide very little assistance
with child-minding. Since the French services facilitate the parents'
income-earning, they help to improve the standard of living for the
country's children. The government's provision and subsidization
of child care also free up money in the family budget for better
food, clothing, and shelter.

In France, the major income-supplementation programs include
family allowances, housing assistance, and cash payments to pregnant women and the parents of young babies. Some of these programs are aimed just at people toward the lower end of the income
distribution; some are available regardless of income. The programs
are not restricted to families in which nobody holds a substantial
job, and they are available to couples, married or unmarried. They
help parents with low-wage jobs maintain a standard higher than
their wages alone would sustain. Less than 10 percent of the French
government's expenditures for income supplementation for families with children are devoted to welfare-like programs—that is, to
sustain parents who do not earn any pay.[5]

In the United States, the situation has been almost precisely the
opposite. A high proportion of the spending has been for aid programs restricted to families with little or no wage income. AFDC is
not designed to raise families with children above the poverty line.
Its purpose is to prevent outright destitution and its consequences—homelessness, starvation, untreated illness, and the tragedy of
penniless mothers forced to give their children into the hands of
strangers. These programs do help single parents avoid destitution.
The Earned Income Tax Credit extends benefits, which are modest,
to parents with jobs, but this benefit accounts for a small proportion of total benefit expenditure. Overall, the American programs
aimed at low-income families help very few couples.

The two countries also provide medical care very differently.
France, like all modern, industrialized countries with the exception
of the United States, has a system of national health insurance,
which functions as part of its social security system and covers virtually all legal residents. With regard to the specific needs of children, a government agency monitors and provides preventive care
to pregnant women and young children. A specialized corps of

public health nurses maintained by the French government is dedicated to monitoring and promoting children's health and welfare. Moreover, unlike Americans, French citizens do not lose their health insurance if they lose or change jobs, or go from welfare to work, or become ill with a disease that is expensive to treat.[6]

In the United States, the situation is more complex. About 71 percent of the population in 1992 was covered by privately provided health insurance, mostly arranged and partly paid for by employers. However, this employer provision is entirely voluntary, and a significant and growing number of employers have opted not to give it.[7] Moreover, employers seldom provide medical benefits to part-time or temporary employees, and the proportion of workers in these categories is growing.[8] So employer provision by no means covers the entire employed population and their dependents. Eleven percent of the population received health insurance from the government through Medicare (for retirees) and Medicaid (mostly for poor families on welfare and the indigent old in nursing homes). This left 18 percent of the population uncovered. American children are less likely to be uncovered than adults: 12 percent had no health insurance coverage in 1992.[9] Most of the children lacking health coverage had parents whose low-wage jobs did not carry health insurance benefits.

The French programs also do a better job of detecting problems of parental ignorance, cruelty, neglect, or incapacity, and mitigating their destructive effects on children. Infants and pre–elementary-school children have regular contact with the employees of the publicly run child-care facilities and are seen by publicly paid physicians and nurses. The likelihood that physical abuse will go undetected, or that a serious physical or mental problem will go untreated, is thereby reduced.

WHAT THESE PROGRAMS COST

Table 2.1 shows the 1991 levels of public expenditure in the two countries for programs that address children's well-being, other than expenditures for elementary, junior high, and high schools.[10] While the quality of schooling strongly affects earnings in adulthood, these nonschool expenditures are the ones most immediately pertinent to children's standard of living and to the extent of childhood poverty.[11] The figures for both France and the United States

TABLE 2.1 SUMMARY OF FRENCH AND U.S. GOVERNMENT
EXPENDITURES FOR CHILDREN'S WELL-BEING, 1991

Type of Expenditure	France Billions of Francs	France Billions of Dollars[a]	United States Billions of Dollars
Child care and development	Fr 63.9	$45.4	$23.9
Provision of care	46.9	33.3	21.6
Cash payment and tax relief to families for child care	17.0	12.1	2.3
Income supplementation	189.0	134.3	89.9
Payments to improve living standards for families with children	139.0	98.8	64.5
Income tax reductions for families with children	50.0	35.5	25.4
Medical care[b]	39.8	51.7	32.1
Public expenditure for medical care for poorest one-quarter of families with children	34.7	45.0	31.5
Preventive medicine	5.1	6.7	0.6
Total	292.7	$231.4	$145.9

Sources: See tables 3.1, 4.1, 5.1, 6.1.

[a] French expenditure translated into dollars of equivalent purchasing power, and then adjusted to take account of the greater number of children in the United States.

[b] Since the ratio of American medical prices to French medical prices is higher than the ratio of prices for other goods, a different conversion factor to dollars is used for medical expenses. See notes to table 5.1.

in table 2.1 include expenditures by states (*départements* in France) and localities, as well as those of the central government.

To allow comparison between the two countries, French expenditure has been converted into dollars of equivalent purchasing power.[12] Also, because the United States is much larger than France, with 4.6 times the number of children, the French figures are multiplied by 4.6 to make them comparable on a per-child basis. The result is presented in the second column of table 2.1, and these numbers are the ones to be compared with actual American government spending for similar or analogous functions. This conversion of French expenditures produces an approximation of what sums the United States would have to spend if it were to establish programs similar to those of the French.

French government spending is higher than U.S. spending in every category.[13] In all, French governmental and quasi-governmental entities spent 293 billion francs for such programs in 1991, the equivalent of more than $231 billion in a country of our size. By comparison, programs for children in the United States cost $146 billion in that year. If Americans were to spend, on a per capita basis, what the French spend on programs for the benefit of children, our government entities would have to lay out about 59 percent more each year than they currently do.[14]

As we have seen, the American programs whose expenditures are tallied in table 2.1, as currently structured, rescue very few American children from poverty. A differently structured and considerably more expensive set of new programs would be necessary if the United States were to provide a decent standard of living for all American children. The substantial amounts we already spend would need to be redirected and augmented to finance those new programs.

The American programs would inevitably differ from the French ones in form and execution, because of differing history, the political power of various interest groups, and differing ideas as to what is acceptable. To give an example, if every child between three and six in the United States were offered a place in a free high-quality nursery school, as they are in France, it is likely that the per-child costs would be substantially different in the two countries. The program set up in the United States would probably depend less than the French one on provision of care in public facilities. Because of an historical lack of public provision, a substantial private nursery-school and day-care industry has grown up in the United States that could not be displaced. The American program would have to involve vouchers that could be used in private centers, some of them profit-making. The cost of vouchers to the government would depend on the staffing patterns and pay scales of these business entities.

Table 2.2 puts the costs of these programs into perspective. In 1991 the French government spent $1.66 on children's programs for every $1.00 of military expenditure. The United States, on the other hand, spent only 44 cents on children for each $1.00 spent on the military. The United States put 8 percent of total government spending at all levels into such programs, while France expended 10 percent of a much higher per-capita amount of government funds. France spent 5 percent of its gross national product on these programs, while the United States spent 3 percent.

TABLE 2.2 GOVERNMENT EXPENDITURES ON CHILDREN'S WELL-BEING
COMPARED WITH OTHER EXPENDITURES FOR THE
UNITED STATES AND FRANCE, 1991

Expenditures	France[a]	United States
Annual government expenditures for	*Billions of Dollars*	
programs for children's well-being	$231	$146
Defense budget	139	331
Total government spending	2,249	1,941
Gross domestic product	4,806	5,611
Government spending on children's		
well-being as a percentage of:	*Percent*	
Defense budget	166%	44%
Total government spending	10	8
Gross domestic product	5	3

Sources: On children's program expenditures, see tables 3.1, 4.1, 5.1, and 6.1. All other data
are from *OECD in Figures* (1993).
[a] French expenditure translated into dollars of equivalent purchasing power, and then
adjusted to take account of the greater number of children in the United States.

The French finance their more generous programs of government benefits with tax rates that are almost half again as high as
taxes in the United States, as table 2.3 shows. They depend far more
heavily than we do on sales taxes and social security taxes, which
seem to be more politically acceptable than the income taxes on
which we depend relatively heavily, although the former are more
regressive. The burden of taxes in France is mitigated by the fact
that French families do not have to use their after-tax income to
purchase services supplied through the public purse, such as child
care and health insurance.

U.S. ATTITUDES TOWARD
"PROGRAMS FOR CHILDREN"

Americans are accustomed to think that the primary beneficiaries
of child care, income supplementation, and medical care programs
are parents, and in particular, mothers, rather than children.[15] One
reason for that attitude is that most of the American programs
focus on families at the bottom of the income scale. Unlike the
French programs "for children," which benefit families up and

TABLE 2.3 TAXATION IN FRANCE AND THE UNITED STATES AS A
PERCENTAGE OF GROSS DOMESTIC PRODUCT (GDP), 1990

Tax	Percentage of GDP	
	France	United States
Personal income taxes	5.2%	10.7%
Corporate income taxes	2.4	2.2
Social security taxes	17.7	8.4
Sales and value-added taxes	12.3	4.9
Other taxes	6.2	3.6
Total	43.7	29.9

Source: OECD in Figures (1993), 42–43.

down the income scale, American programs go to the least respected members of the population, those whose behavior is regarded as the least prudent and who appear to be making the least effort to extricate themselves from poverty. (That many African-American families who receive the benefits have had the cards stacked against them by racial discrimination does not usually enter into the discussion.) In contrast to the French, who generally regard income supplements as deserved and sensible help to struggling families, Americans tend to view these programs as necessary but regrettable assistance to "people who sit in the wagon instead of helping to pull it."[16] The spotlight often plays on the deficiencies of these adults rather than on the needs of their children when American programs for child well-being are discussed.

The exceptions are the American tax breaks for the middle- and upper-class families with children—exemptions for dependent children and deductions for child-care expenses. These tax breaks are not generally considered part of a broad system of programs to help children. They are not perceived to be in the same category as AFDC, partly because the groups who receive them do not overlap with AFDC recipients—a family belongs to one group or the other, not both. Many Americans see tax breaks as a "deserved" return of a family's "own income," but they do not see AFDC cash payments in the same way.

Another reason that many Americans might fail to classify AFDC as part of a system that "helps children" is that it is widely suspected of contributing to bad parenting, inducing laziness or irresponsible behavior in adults, to the ultimate detriment of their children, and encouraging people to become parents who cannot care for children adequately and without help from the taxpayers.[17] Another is that most people understand that AFDC does not eliminate poverty; many recipients still live a miserably deprived existence. Given that reality, the statement that—school aside—welfare is America's most important and expensive program benefiting children, sounds like a joke. The fact that it is the truth is a clear indication that the "benefits" to our children are seriously wanting.

A system that Americans would recognize as helping all its children to lead decent lives would probably have to share some of the features of the French system summarized above. It would give major help to large numbers of parents, not just non-jobholders. It would give the most help to those who earn low wages, through income supplementation and subsidies for child care. It would help all families who have children with access to medical insurance and the financing for it. Such a system would spend large amounts on services going directly to children. (One advantage of direct services to children rather than cash to parents is that the parents cannot be accused of having children in order to receive such benefits.) It would create fewer perverse incentives and encourage parents to work as a means of escaping poverty. The system would have to contain an AFDC-like provision to help parents who are mentally or physically disabled, who have disabled children, or who are temporarily unemployed. But that component would be much smaller as a share of the whole program, and fewer families would need to benefit from it. That revamped set of programs would more easily be recognized as directed at children's well-being than the present AFDC-plus-food-stamps-plus-Medicaid package the United States now has in place.

Resistance to these proposals is relatively easy to predict. First, detractors will point to the cost, suggesting that the United States cannot afford these programs. Indeed, there is no current discussion of creating an American program along the French lines, since the prevailing wisdom is that there is "no money" for anything new.

Second, the debate will focus on whether the government should be involved in providing child care. Programs that function primarily to keep children safe, happy, and healthy while their parents work are controversial in the United States. Some people believe that a mother's full-time care in the preschool years is indispensable to a child's happiness and healthy development.[18] The claim that day care harms children is not supported by the bulk of the systematic research, but it continues to resonate, in part because many of those who hold it are highly invested in seeing women return to their traditional roles.[19] People with this point of view argue that free or subsidized child care would not help children, and would actually do them a disservice because it tempts mothers to get jobs.

At the same time, it is widely acknowledged by many of the same people that all-mother care has not produced satisfactory results for one large group of American children—those whose mothers receive welfare. One might argue that, whatever effect home-based care has on middle-class children, better outcomes for poor children require some form of preschool experience.

Perhaps more crucially, whatever we think about mothers staying at home or going out to work, the reality is that mothers in many families must work outside the home to support their children. In practice a decent existence for the children of single mothers is possible only under two conditions: (1) the family has income from wages, and (2) the family does not have to set aside a large portion of those wages for buying child care and health care. Thus, the provision or subsidy of child care by the government has an indispensable role to play in pushing single-mother families above the poverty line. In addition to the substantial financial benefits that government-subsidized child care may confer on the family, a high-quality child-care center can provide a safe, comfortable, nurturing daytime environment for a child from a marginalized group. In such a setting, the child may derive vital developmental and health benefits that may be unavailable at home.

For a time, there was discussion by Republicans of a total cessation of welfare,[20] and even discussion of establishing orphanages for the children whose parents would have to give them up as a result. Now, the current Republican plan is simply to offer a thinner soup to welfare families—consisting of decentralized control of welfare, reduced benefit levels, and an end to the guarantee of benefits to all eligible families. Although the Democrats resist, they offer no distinct plan of their own.

In addition, we have heard much preaching of "family values." Even if the curtailment of nonmarital sex and a lower divorce rate could reduce both the number of single-parent families and child poverty, such a large-scale change in social practices is unlikely to occur as a result of preaching or any other means. On the other hand, the political feasibility of establishing a system to help families with children—one that would greatly reduce the poverty epidemic among American children—is as dim as it has been since 1929. It would cost a great deal of additional money. However, the models abroad demonstrate that it is feasible and that we would know how to do it.

✤ PART II ✤

French Programs For Child Well-Being

✣ CHAPTER 3 ✣

Government Child-Care Programs in France

THE FRENCH NATIONAL and local governments give parents a great deal of help in caring for their pre-elementary school children. The government runs a system of free nursery schools and provides thousands of highly subsidized places in day-care centers for infants and toddlers up to age three whose mothers have jobs. In addition to running and paying for extensive child-care facilities, the French government also gives cash benefits and tax breaks to parents who buy child care on the private market. The cost to French taxpayers of these facilities, benefits, and subsidies added up to 64 billion francs in 1991.[1] (See table 3.1.) That is the equivalent, for a country the size of the United States, of $45 billion a year. Despite this expenditure, the French have long wanted to provide still more places for infant and toddler care and are working vigorously to accomplish that. Between 1982 and 1990, the number of places in publicly provided care for children under age three increased by 55 percent.[2]

Further, the help that French parents get with children's care and development extends well beyond the preschool years. The public elementary schools in France enforce high national standards. About 45 percent of children going through the school system emerge with a baccalaureate degree from a *lycée*—a free public secondary school with academic programs that equal or exceed in excellence the best private education available in the United States.[3]

27

TABLE 3.1 SUMMARY OF FRENCH GOVERNMENT EXPENDITURES
ON CHILD CARE, 1991

Child-care Expenditures	Billions of Francs	Billions of Dollars[a]
Provision of care	Fr 46.897	$33.329
Infant care	7.209	5.123
Nursery schools	37.316	26.520
Other government-provided care	2.372	1.686
Other benefits to families for child care	16.993	12.077
Unemployed parent's allowance (APE)	5.923	4.209
Nanny subsidy (AGED)	0.279	0.198
Paid parental leave	9.257	6.579
Subsidies for licensed family day care (AFEAMA)	0.534	0.380
Income tax reduction for child-care expenses	1.000	0.711
Total spending on child care	63.890	45.406

Sources: Provision of care: see tables 3.3, 3.5, 3.8. Income tax reduction for child-care expenses: Centre d'Étude des Revenus et des Coûts, *Politique familiale et dimension de la famille* (Paris: La Documentation Française, 1992), 29. Paid parental leave: Commission des Comptes de la Sécurité Sociale: Rapport, *Les comptes de la sécurité sociale* (Paris: La Documentation Française, July 1992), 257. Other benefits data from *CAF statistiques; prestations familiales, 1991* (Paris: Caisse Nationale des Allocations Familiales, n.d.), 120.
[a] French expenditure translated into dollars of equivalent purchasing power, and then adjusted to take account of the greater number of children in the United States.

Lycées are open to French children from all income strata on a competitive basis. As a result, well-off parents who want high standards for their children do not have to pay for private education; lower-income parents do not have to watch their talented children languish in schools that are inadequate for them. In addition, supervised recreational programs for school-age children for the after-school hours, and during summers and school vacations, subsidized by the government, are common. Free tuition in public universities, including medical and law school, relieves French parents of a heavy financial burden that American parents must face.

This chapter examines the various child-care programs that France offers its families. As we will see, the wealth of resources available to French families contrasts sharply with the struggles over cost, quality, and availability of child care facing American families.

NURSERY SCHOOLS: *ÉCOLES MATERNELLES*

From the American point of view, the most striking component of France's government programs for children is the *école maternelle* (nursery school or infant school),[4] for which parents pay no fees, regardless of their income. Children can enroll as soon as they are toilet-trained and attend until they enter first grade. Thus, children commonly attend these nursery schools for three-and-a-half of their six preprimary years. With rare temporary exceptions, all children who apply for enrollment can be accommodated.[5] For poor families, these schools provide a level of care and nurturance they could not possibly afford in the private market. The availability of high-quality, free child care also means that poor women who become mothers can work to support their children.

Nursery schools have a long history in France. Early prototypes, which were intended to serve the children of poor working parents, were established under religious auspices before the Revolution of 1789. By the 1820s, the first public nursery schools were established, and their number grew rapidly thereafter. Free public primary education was guaranteed to all children by law in 1881, and at that time the *écoles maternelles* were formally established as an integral part of the free public educational system.[6] The *écoles maternelles* were declared in a law of 1887 to be "establishments where children receive their first education, where the two sexes receive in common the care that promotes their physical, moral and intellectual development."[7]

As the name implies, the *école maternelle* is considered a school, not merely a custodial caretaker. They are under the aegis of the central government's Ministry of Education, which pays the teachers and administrators, while the local governments pay for the auxiliary personnel, the buildings, and building upkeep. Private nursery schools, mostly sponsored by religious organizations, are partially subsidized by government funds and attended by 12 percent of the children in nursery school.[8]

Many of the public nursery schools are in new, bright, spacious, specially designed buildings, kept to a high standard of maintenance and cleanliness. They are an obvious part of the urban landscape in France. When a new one is to be built, an architectural competition is held to pick the best design. The contrast with the church basements in which many American day-care centers operate is often dramatic.

In 1991, the public nursery schools in France served 2.2 million children, a remarkably high proportion of young children in France, as table 3.2 shows.[9] Between the ages of three and six, virtually all children go to *écoles maternelles*. Since children become

TABLE 3.2 PERCENTAGE OF FRENCH CHILDREN ATTENDING NURSERY
SCHOOL, BY AGE, 1960–91

Age of Child (Years)	1960	1970	1980	1991
Two	10%	18%	36%	36%
Three	36	61	90	99
Four	63	87	100	100
Five	91	100	100	100

Sources: Data for 1960–80 from Ministère de l'Éducation Nationale de la Jeunesse et des Sports, *Repères et références statistiques sur les enseignements et la formation* (Paris, 1990), 97. Data for 1991 from *Contours et caractères; les enfants de moins de 6 ans* (Paris: Institut National de la Statistique et des Études Économiques, 1992), 87.

toilet-trained at about two-and-a-half, we can estimate that about 70 percent of the toilet-trained children between two and three currently attend, up from about 20 percent in 1960. Although a child may attend half-time, most go full-time: 8:30 A.M. to 4:30 P.M. Coordinated before- and after-school care is available for very low fees.[10] The closest analogy to the *école maternelle* on the American scene—in terms of its open access, low cost, and developmental emphasis—is public kindergarten, which enrolls most children, but only in their fifth year and mostly on a half-day basis.

As in the United States, it is common for French mothers who do not hold jobs to send their children to nursery school. In France, virtually all of them do so by the time the child reaches the age of three. It is understood that the primary mission of the nursery schools is to help the children develop. Sending the child thus becomes the duty of a good parent; and, in fact, the *école maternelle* is one of the most popular government programs in France, if conversations with parents, bureaucrats, and politicians are any guide.

Like the country's public elementary schools, the public nursery schools in France do not operate on Wednesday and operate a half-day on Saturday. This practice was established by an agreement between the government and the French Catholic hierarchy, and provides a free day in the middle of the week for children to receive religious education (usually part-day), if the parents so desire. This schedule obviously creates a problem for working parents and crimps weekend excursions by families. Public authorities are under considerable pressure to alter it. Alternative means of care are provided in public facilities on Wednesdays.

Each nursery school class is supervised by a professional teacher, who is required to have the same qualifications as an elementary school teacher—the equivalent of a master's degree—and a teaching aide is available for every two teachers. A large, urban nursery school consisting of seven classrooms and enrolling about two hundred children might have a director, seven teachers, four teachers' aides, and eight part-time recreation leaders for before- and after-school care and lunch-time supervision. In addition, such a school might have four kitchen aides, a building superintendent, and the part-time services of a professional cook.[11] In the United States, a typical nursery school or day-care center for preschoolers would serve sixty-eight children and employ about eleven teachers and aides.[12]

Class size in a French public nursery school is twenty-eight but absences due to illness reduce the number attending on any given day to an average of twenty-four.[13] That works out to sixteen children per adult in the classroom, counting the teacher and the half-time teacher aide. In the United States, child-care experts consider an adult–child ratio of 1:9 to be crucial to providing high-quality care; U.S. preschools abide by this finding. However, a group of American experts on day care who observed French child-care facilities in 1989 concluded that, despite the larger number of children per adult, the quality of the *écoles maternelles* was as high as or higher than the best and highest-cost American day-care centers.[14] More systematic studies of teacher-child interactions confirm this impression.[15] One study concluded that the teacher training in France, which encourages teachers to carefully plan daily activities and constantly monitor the children, explained the good results.[16]

In 1991 the starting annual salary for a teacher was 92,134 francs ($14,153) a year, plus free housing (or an annual tax-free housing allowance) and the regular fringe benefits of government employees such as pensions, vacations, and tenure.[17] His or her salary rises to a maximum of 189,192 francs ($29,061) per year.[18] Given the job stability associated with the civil service, the pay is apparently sufficient to attract stable, well-educated people to these jobs, in sharp contrast to the situation in American day care, where employee turnover is high and the employees are often ill-educated, have no special training in childhood education, and are paid the minimum wage.[19]

Table 3.3 presents government expenditures for nursery schools in France in 1991. In that year, 37 billion francs were spent, the equivalent of $27 billion for a country the size of the United States. The Ministry of Education estimated the cost of keeping a child enrolled for a year at 15,600 francs (equivalent in terms of purchasing power to $2,396).[20] In the United States, keeping a child for a year in a high-quality day-care center or nursery school would cost parents more than $5,000.[21]

The school activities at the *écoles maternelles* include painting, singing, dancing, games, sports, and field trips. The walls of the rooms and corridors are full of art posters. Along with physical activities, activities to refine sensory perception and promote effective language use are emphasized, as are "activities having as their aim the formation of the beginning of moral habits."[22] Both self-expression and correct behavior are taught.[23]

Another important item on the *école maternelle's* agenda is exposing the children to the traditional French culture—making "French people" out of them. For example, I observed on a site visit a professional chef prepare the children's lunch from scratch. The children were served on china dishes, with the food elegantly arranged. The lunch started off with Camembert cheese, which a young child might not normally eat. The cook explained to me that the children "tolerated" the cheese better at the beginning of the meal than at the end. Had it been served to them at the end of the meal, they might have left it untasted. Served at the beginning of

TABLE 3.3 FRENCH GOVERNMENT SPENDING FOR NURSERY SCHOOLS, 1991

Spending	Billions of Francs	Billions of Dollars[a]
Current expenses		
Teaching	Fr 31.152	$22.139
Food	1.939	1.378
Administration	0.872	0.620
Other expenses	2.095	1.489
Capital expenses	1.259	0.895
Total	37.316	26.520

Source: Ministère de l'Éducation Nationale et de la Culture, *Le compte de l'éducation: résultats 1987 à 1991* (Paris, 1992), 109–11.
[a] French expenditure translated into dollars of equivalent purchasing power, and then adjusted to take account of the greater number of children in the United States.

the meal, when they were hungry, some of them tried it, thus ensuring another generation of cheese-eating French.

As a school, the *école maternelle* works to get the four- and five-year-olds ready for the first grade. In the French educational system, passing the first grade requires mastery of a considerable body of skills, and many children are required to repeat it. Table 3.4 shows that attendance at nursery school significantly improves first-grade performance. Of children from poorer backgrounds who have not attended an *école maternelle*, over half fail the first grade. Four years of preschool attendance for such children cut their first grade failure rate in half.[24] Children from more affluent backgrounds are also helped to pass.

An effort is made in the *école maternelle* to diagnose any physical, mental, or emotional problems a child may have and to detect abuse. A recently instituted program aims to provide a checkup for all four-year-old enrollees by the physicians from the *Protection Maternelle et Infantile* (PMI). Children with problems are directed to appropriate treatment and followed up carefully.

The *écoles maternelles* are particularly helpful to children from minority and deprived backgrounds or from dysfunctional families. The safe, well-lit, clean, and nicely decorated schools provide a place where children can be away for many of their waking hours from the problems that face them at home and in their neighborhoods, and in the company of well-educated adults trained to assist their development. Most of the poor urban children of pre-elementary school age in the United States have no such place of refuge.

Like the United States, France has sizable ethnic minorities, many of whose members are not well integrated into mainstream

TABLE 3.4 PERCENTAGE OF FRENCH CHILDREN REPEATING THE FIRST
GRADE, BY TIME SPENT IN NURSERY SCHOOL

Occupation of Parents	None	1 Year	2 Years	3 Years	4 Years
Professional and executive	a	11.6%	10.9%	8.0%	4.6%
Skilled workers	a	25.1	21.8	17.5	14.8
Unskilled workers	53.7%	41.4	38.1	32.6	27.0

Source: Ministère de l'Éducation Nationale, "Durée de l'enseignement préscolaire et déroulement de la scolarité ultérieure, premiers résultats du panel 80," in *Note d'Information 82-09 du Service des Études Informatiques et Statistiques* (Paris, 1982).
a There are virtually no children in this category.

culture and the economy.[25] Considerable numbers of people from less-developed countries, particularly Algeria and the formerly French colonies of sub-Saharan Africa have immigrated to France, and about 10 percent of the children in French schools are foreign nationals.[26] In addition, many French-born children are of foreign parentage. The nursery schools—especially their availability over the course of several formative years—serve an important role in introducing immigrant children to the French language and culture, getting them ready for school, and in the longer run, getting them ready to participate successfully in the economy. By contrast, the public kindergartens in the United States, which are the closest analogs to the *écoles maternelles*, typically provide only one year of half-days.

As in the United States, some French people resent these immigrants. Some right-wing local politicians, whose governments have to pay in part for child-care services delivered to immigrants, have agitated against providing them with benefits. However, benefits relating to children are available to all who legally live in France.[27] In at least one well-publicized case, a local mayor attempted to bar the children of a Senegalese man who had four wives and twenty-eight children from the town's *école maternelle*. The school director, who reports to the Ministry of Education in Paris, refused to obey the mayor's edict, explaining that the children could not learn French if they were excluded.[28] The view among government officials is that the children of immigrants now in France are destined to grow up there and stay there, so the more acculturated they are, the better it will be for the country and for them. While the French educational authorities defend the right of immigrants' children to the benefits, they are not shy in demanding that these children conform to French cultural standards.[29]

If the United States were to decide to help families—particularly low-wage families—by providing child care, the French system of *écoles maternelles* would provide one possible model for the core of a new system, one with many very attractive characteristics. Since an American kindergarten class and an *école maternelle* class share many features, it could be done by greatly expanding the number of full-day public kindergarten places and making them available, along with after-school care, to children from three to five. In the classes attended by the younger children, activities would have to be altered appropriately, and teacher-student ratios raised. Kindergarten teachers in the United States, like the teachers in the *écoles maternelles*, have credentials similar to those who teach in the higher grades, far better than their counterparts in day-care centers. Thanks to their far higher pay and fringe benefits, public kindergarten teachers have the low turnover rates that researchers have found to be highly correlated with quality care. Typically, those who work in American facilities for preschool children, with the exception of kindergarten teachers, have low pay and high turnover rates.[30]

The difficulties of expanding kindergartens to achieve a child-care system like that of the *écoles maternelles* are mostly political—the opposition to the increased government expenditure, the disinclination of nongovernmental child-care centers to lose a large share of their market, and the determined opposition of those who want to see mothers (except for welfare mothers) retreat from the job market and return to caring for their own children in their own home. In thinking about the practical problem of solving child poverty, the subject of chapters 7 and 8, these political difficulties must be factored in when deciding what policies to advocate.

FULL-TIME INFANT AND TODDLER CARE: *CRÈCHES*

Crèches—publicly supported centers for the care of infants and toddlers in France—currently can accommodate about 20 percent of the children under age three whose mothers hold jobs.[31] Like the nursery schools, these centers are of a generally high quality.[32] The infant care centers are supported by local governments, with modest subsidies provided by the national government. Private, nonprofit groups that set up such centers can get public money to help with costs. Because the care of young babies requires a high ratio of staff to children, these facilities are extremely costly to run. Unlike the *écoles maternelles*, the *crèches* charge fees, which are graduated according to family income. Infant care can take various forms, resulting in some cost differences among centers. (Table 3.5 gives these differing costs and the numbers of children currently enrolled nationally.)

CRÈCHE COLLECTIVE

The most common form of infant care is the *crèche collective*, the rough equivalent of the American day-care center for children

TABLE 3.5 GOVERNMENT-SUBSIDIZED FACILITIES IN FRANCE FOR FULL-TIME INFANT CARE, 1991

Facility	Number of Places	Daily Cost	Minimum Daily Fee	Maximum Daily Fee	Average Daily Fee	Annual Cost to Government (Millions)[a]
				Francs		
Regular day-care center (*crèche collective*)	93,900	Fr 286	Fr 40	Fr 140	Fr 65	Fr 4,567
Supervised family day care (*crèche familiale*)	61,300	217	40	140	65	2,050
Cooperative center (*crèche mini/parentale*)	20,700	175	20	100	45	592
Total	175,900					7,209
				Dollars		
Regular day-care center (*crèche collective*)	93,900	$43.93	$6.14	$21.51	$9.98	$3,246
Supervised family day care (*crèche familiale*)	61,300	33.33	6.14	21.51	9.98	1,457
Cooperative center (*crèche mini/parentale*)	20,700	26.88	3.07	15.36	6.91	421
Total	175,900					5,124

Sources: Information on costs and fees from *Créer un mode d'accueil pour les enfants de 0 à 6 ans: guide pratique* (Lyon: Conseil Petite Enfance du Rhône, 1992). Information on availability of places in 1990 from *Contours et caractères; les enfants de moins de 6 ans* (Paris: Institut National de la Statistique et des Études Economiques, 1992), 75; projected to 1991 using historic rates of growth. Estimates of government costs made by author under assumption government bears 75 percent of total cost.

[a] In the conversion to dollar amounts, the difference in population size was taken into account.

36

under age three. Typically, a center cares for forty to sixty infants from two months to three years old. One caregiver is available for every five infants, and one for every eight toddlers. Additional staff help with cleaning and food preparation. The average number of children per caregiver during any given day is lower because of absenteeism. In 1991 such a *crèche* spent 234 francs ($36) per day to accommodate a baby. In most centers, children can be dropped off as early as seven o'clock in the morning, and picked up as late as seven o'clock in the evening.

Careful attention is paid to the building the *crèche* occupies. To ensure safety, for example, the outer edge of the doors are sheathed in hollow rubber tubing, so that a slamming door will not injure a child's fingers.

Table 3.6 presents a sample operating budget for a small *crèche collective*. It operates 220 days a year and is designed to enroll twenty children, with an average of eighteen (90 percent) expected to be present on a typical day (3,960 child-days per year).[33] The budget covers two child-care specialists, three lower-level caregivers, for a ratio of 3.6 children per caregiver. In addition, there are service personnel to help with cleaning and food preparation. Cost and price data are as follows:

	Francs	Dollar Equivalents
Cost per child-year	Fr 51,467	$7,906
Cost per child-day	234	36
Average daily fee paid by parents	65	10
Annual income at which parent of one child would pay full cost	520,000	79,877

The director of the *crèche* will be a *puéricultrice*, a member of a French child-care profession that does not have an American equivalent. The *puéricultrice* has the training of a registered nurse or a midwife and takes a year of additional training in the administration of infant care. Before she can head a *crèche*, she needs an additional five years of professional experience. The budget also calls for an *éducatrice de jeunes enfants*, someone with a baccalaureate (high-level liberal arts) degree from a *lycée* and two additional years of special training, which includes theoretical work and thirty-six weeks of practical experience. The duties of the *éducatrice* are

TABLE 3.6 BUDGET OF A FRENCH DAY-CARE CENTER (*CRÈCHE COLLECTIVE*) CAPABLE OF ENROLLING TWENTY CHILDREN UP TO AGE THREE, 1991

| | For Individual Workers | | | | Total Cost for All Workers | |
| | Salary Net of Social Security | | Social Security Payroll Taxes | | | |
Costs	Francs	Dollars	Francs	Dollars	Francs	Dollars
Personnel (number)						
Puéricultrice (1)	Fr 117,119	$17,999	Fr 52,703	$8,096	Fr 169,822	$26,086
Teacher of young children (1)	106,035	16,288	47,716	7,330	153,751	23,618
Aides to *puéricultrice* (3)	84,976	13,053	38,239	5,874	369,645	56,781
Service workers (1.5)	84,976	13,053	38,239	5,874	184,822	28,391
Total personnel costs	—	—	—	—	878,040	134,876
Rent					48,000	7,373
Food					59,400	9,124
Training					10,000	1,536
Utilities					18,000	2,765
Other					15,900	2,442
Total costs					1,029,340	158,117

Source: Créer un mode d'accueil pour les enfants de 0 à 6 ans: guide pratique (Lyon: Conseil Petite Enfance du Rhône, 1992).

38

to survey on a daily basis the physical state of the children, to watch over their security, to establish the emotional and relational climate [of the *crèche*], to help the children to surmount tensions and conflicts, to seek for the children activities that favor both autonomy and psychomotor development, and to introduce to the group the world around them, especially in the case where the children have been deprived of a normal living situation.[34]

The mandated staffing pattern in a government-provided or supervised *crèche* requires that at least half of the child-care auxiliaries have a year of training in a specialized school run by the central government. The curriculum includes classes in child care and development and practical experience. A *crèche* has an on-call pediatrician attached to it, whose salary is covered by the local public budget for preventive medicine. It can care for mildly ill children.

The salaries included in the budget in table 3.6, especially for the top two positions, are very modest by American standards for people with equivalent training.[35] A registered nurse in the United States, for example, averaged $33,000 a year in 1991. However, in France, tuition for the training for these posts is heavily supported by the government, as are the trainees' living expenses.

The planned cost (in equivalent dollars) of operating the small *crèche* for a year works out to $158,117, or $7,906 per child enrolled. The fees charged to a family depend on its income, the number of children in the family, and the number of its children using the service. As shown in table 3.7, the poorest families pay only token amounts. For one-child families in the middle of the income range, the fee is assessed at 12 percent of family income. For two-child families, the fee per child is lowered to 10 percent of family income. Even fairly well-off families pay considerably less than the cost of providing the services. A family with one child would not have to pay the full cost unless its income exceeded $80,000 a year. On average, parents' fees account for 25 percent of the center's revenue. Subventions from the central government social security funds and from the municipality pay for 19 and 56 percent, respectively.

CRÈCHES FAMILIALES

The high cost to the government of providing care in a *crèche collective* has led to the formation of the *crèches familiales*— each consisting of about fifteen licensed and trained "family day care" providers, who take up to three children into their homes and who

TABLE 3.7 CHARGES PER DAY BY PUBLIC INFANT CARE CENTERS FOR FULL-TIME CARE FOR A CHILD UNDER THREE, BY FAMILY INCOME, 1991

Family's Monthly Income	One-Child Family	Two-Child Family	Three-Child Family or Two Children in Care
	Francs		
Fr 4,500	Fr 27	Fr 22	Fr 16
8,500	50	42	31
16,500	99	82	61
35,500	213	177	133
	Dollars		
$681	$4.15	$3.38	$2.46
1,286	7.68	6.45	4.76
2,496	15.21	12.60	9.37
5,371	32.72	27.19	20.43

Source: CAFAL Action Sociale, "Le barème des participations familiales: la mensualisation" (Paris, 1991).

are supervised by a *puéricultrice*. The latter visits each provider periodically, gives advice, keeps them up to performance standards, and inspects to see that they are following sanitary regulations. As with the *crèche collective*, a pediatrician is on call. The *crèche familiale* thus combines some of the best features of both home care and center care, at a lower cost than the latter. The child is cared for by a single individual in a noninstitutional setting, without being exposed to noise and infections from large numbers of other children. The professional supervision is supposed to result in sanitation and safety that are on a par with those of a *crèche collective*.

The families that send their children to a *crèche familiale* pay the organizing body the same fees they would pay to have their child in a *crèche collective*, which means that the lower-income families are highly subsidized. The administration of the *crèche familiale* pays the day-care providers twice the minimum wage. American parents, many of whom prefer family day care to center care, do not have the option of choosing a form like the *crèche familiale*, which combines small size with rigorous supervision of the provider by a health-care professional. Nor do American parents get the benefit of the subsidies that the *crèche familiale* receives.

Other types of full-time, public infant-care facilities include the *crèche parentale*, for which the American equivalent would be the cooperative day-care center, and *mini-crèches*, which are small versions of the *crèches collectives*, located in an apartment house or some other institution.

✤

Places in publicly subsidized *crèches* are generally not available to children who have a non-jobholding parent at home. Exceptions are made when there is a special need—for example, when a parent is an alcoholic, is addicted to drugs, is having mental problems, or is suspected of child abuse, but where the authorities are attempting to keep the child with its parents.

Unlike the nursery schools, the number of places currently available in France's infant-care centers is far lower than the number of places that are demanded at current prices. Because of this situation, political patronage sometimes influences whose child gets a given slot.[36] The central government offers substantial subsidies to stimulate municipalities and private groups to establish new infant-care facilities under a so-called *Contrat-Enfance* program.[37] However, the high cost of running these facilities has deterred more rapid progress in setting up new ones.

PART-TIME CHILD-CARE FACILITIES

The French maintain a considerable variety of publicly supported child-care facilities that take children part-time, or temporarily, or on short notice and that fill in when the regular facilities are not operating.

Garderies périscolaires (before- and after-school care centers), managed and subsidized by municipalities, are available in most urban localities for children who go to nursery or elementary school but who need care outside of regular school hours. Many of them are located in the school whose children they serve. Or they may be set up in the home of an *assistante maternelle* who is attached to a *crèche familiale*, or in other suitable locations. In these latter cases, they deliver the children to school when it opens and pick them up after it closes. A *garderie périscolaire* is run by a trained and licensed child-care worker.

This coordinated care for the hours before and after school is available for 5–15 francs (77 cents to $2.30) per hour per child, according to income. Parents may drop off their children as early as seven o'clock A.M. and pick them up as late as seven o'clock P.M. In the United States, some public schools do provide organized after-school care, but these arrangements are not as common as they are in France. As a result, there are many latch-key children—children who spend their after-school hours at home alone, with no supervision.[38]

Haltes-garderies (drop-in child-care centers) are without parallel in the United States. Their main function is to take care of children under age three for a few hours on short notice. Such facilities allow a mother who stays home to take time off for personal business, or perhaps just take a respite from child care.[39] Although most of the places are reserved for children on unscheduled, occasional visits, some children come part-time on a regular schedule. This allows a mother to hold a part-time job, or it provides a transition period for the child soon to go to nursery school.

Alain Norvez, a leading observer of French policy toward young children, remarks that *haltes-garderies* are not taken as seriously as they deserve to be; the French public tends to see these facilities as deluxe "parking places" for children while the mother goes to the hairdresser or plays tennis. Norvez sees them, on the contrary, as filling a real and urgent need. Children benefit from the improvement in their mothers' disposition when they can take a break. Children also need a break from their mothers, and it does them good to be at least occasionally in the company of others their own age. For an immigrant mother, who may be acculturated to keeping the child at home and avoiding the use of public child-care facilities, the occasional short-term use of an *halte-garderie* may make her more comfortable about sending her child to a nursery school and may allow the child to begin to learn French and acclimate to French cultural norms.[40]

An *halte-garderie* with places for eighteen children—two-thirds for drop-ins and one-third for regularly scheduled part-timers— might be supervised by an *éducatrice de jeunes enfants* assisted by a child-care auxiliary and one or two service personnel. The daily operating cost of such a facility in 1991 was 195 francs ($31) per child. Parents' fees would cover about one-quarter of the costs and would range from 2 to 10 francs (31 cents to $1.54) per hour, depending on the parents' income.[41]

Centres de loisirs (neighborhood leisure centers) receive children when the schools are closed: after school hours, on Wednesdays, on the many religious and civic holidays, during the Christmas vacation, during winter and spring school breaks, and during summer vacations. They serve children aged two years old and up. There is one staff person for each eight children; in each center, at least half of the staff members must have received specific training for this function. The cost of operating these centers (as of 1989) was 70 to 90 francs ($10.75 to $13.82, 1991 dollars) per day per child. Again, parents pay 2 to 10 francs (31 cents to $1.54) per hour. In addition, the government runs summer camps for children four years old and up. The children go for three weeks at a time, mostly in July and August.

A new kind of center is the *relais parental* (loosely translated as "stopover home" or "family relief home"), a residential facility that stays open around the clock to receive children whose families are experiencing severe, generally temporary, difficulties. This facility avoids a formal and permanent out-of-home placement for children who need a place to live for a brief period. Couples having marital difficulties and single mothers who are having a difficult relationship with their babies are typical users. The managers of one such facility close to Paris remarked that their establishment takes the place of a grandparent or a kind neighbor. Some parents use the facility repeatedly, popping the child in when the going gets tough, perhaps once a week or once a month. The cost to the family came to 33 francs (about $5) per day per child in 1994.[42]

A spirit of experimentation has produced a number of other new forms of centers for children: *accueil parents-enfants,* which features parent-child play sessions to prepare the child for a full-fledged child-care center; *caravane halte-garderie,* a child-care facility set up in a bus that travels to different neighborhoods; *atelier d'éveil,* literally a "workshop for awakening," which offers a half-day of physical, creative, and artistic experience, presumably to youngsters not enrolled in nursery schools; and *ludothèque animation* (translated as "fun and games"), a facility that parents and children attend together.[43]

The parents, the municipalities, and the social security fund—the *Caisse des Allocations Familiale* (CAF)—share these child-care costs. Table 3.8 summarizes estimated spending by the government on part-time child care in 1991, through the CAF and the municipalities.

TABLE 3.8 GOVERNMENT-SUBSIDIZED FACILITIES FOR PART-TIME CHILD CARE IN FRANCE, 1991

Facility (Number of Places)	Daily Cost Per Child		Minimum Hourly Fee		Maximum Hourly Fee		Annual Cost to Government	
	Francs	Dollars	Francs	Dollars	Francs	Dollars	Billions of Francs	Billions of Dollars[a]
Occasional care facilities (*haltes-garderies*) (54,991)	Fr 195	$30.57	Fr 2	$0.31	Fr 10	$1.54	Fr 0.903	$0.642
Jardins d'enfance (11,939)	199	30.57	b	b	b	b	0.196	0.139
Before- and after-school care (*garderies périscolaires*)	199	5.38	5	0.17	15	2.30	0.350	0.249
Leisure centers (1.7 million children averaging 44 days per year)	80	12.29	2	0.31	10	1.54	0.330	0.234
Vacation camps (567,700 child-days)	b	b	b	b	b	b	0.593	0.422
Total							2.372	1.686

Sources: Information on costs and fees from *Créer un mode d'accueil pour les enfants de 0 à 6 ans: guide pratique* (Lyon: Conseil Petite Enfance du Rhône, 1992). Information on availability of places from *Contours et caractères; les enfants de moins de 6 ans* (Paris: Institut National de la Statistique et des Études Économiques, 1992). Government cost of *garderies périscolaires* from "L'accueil temporaire du jeune enfant dans la politique d'action sociale familiale de l'institution . . . aujourd'hui," *CNAF Action Sociale* (January 1993). Government cost of vacation camps is CAF expenditure for 1987 given in *CAF statistiques; action sociale, [19]85–86-87* (Paris: Caisse Nationale des Allocations Familiales, 1991), projected to 1991. Other estimates of government costs made by author under assumption government bears 75 percent of total cost.

[a] French expenditure translated into dollars of equivalent purchasing power, and then adjusted to take account of the greater number of children in the United States.

[b] Data not available.

ASSISTANCE TO PARENTS WHO USE PRIVATE CARE

The French government also provides financial help to parents with infants who do not use government-supported infant-care facilities. These programs involved French government expenditures in 1991 of 17 billion francs, the equivalent of $12 billion for a country the size of the United States. The expenditure on individual programs is tallied in table 3.1. These programs help mothers who stay home with their infants, and mothers with jobs who buy private care for their young children.

About 60 percent of mothers who have children under the age of three hold jobs in France, compared with about 50 percent in the United States.[44] As table 3.9 shows, only 11.5 percent of the children up to age three whose mothers hold a job were cared for in a *crèche collective*, 24.3 percent were in licensed family day care, and 11.5 percent of the children had entered an *école maternelle*. Forty-one percent were cared for by family members in their own homes or elsewhere. Only 7.3 percent were reported to be in unlicensed care.[45]

TABLE 3.9 HOW CHILDREN UNDER THREE WERE CARED FOR IN
FRANCE, 1990

Type of Care	Mothers With Jobs	Mothers Without Jobs
Cared for at home by		
Mother	18.3%	86.4%
Other family member	9.2	0.5
Other	3.9	0.2
Cared for out of the home by		
Crèche	11.5	0.7
École maternelle	11.5	10.4
Licensed *assistante maternelle*[a]	24.3	0.3
Unlicensed caretaker	7.3	0.2
Family member	13.8	0.5
Total	100.0	100.0

Source: Contours et caractères; les enfants de moins de 6 ans (Paris: Institut National de la Statistique et des Études Économiques, 1992), 71.
[a] Includes *assistantes maternelles* who are connected to *crèches familiales*, who care for about 7.5 percent of the children of mothers with jobs. See table 3.5.

Paid Parental Leave: ASSURANCE MATERNITÉ

A woman giving birth to her first or second child is entitled to sixteen weeks of paid maternity leave, six weeks before the birth and ten weeks after. When she has a third child, she gets twenty-six weeks of paid leave. The employer cannot require her to work during the two weeks before the birth and the six weeks after. The employer does not have the right to discharge a woman during her pregnancy and must accept her back after her maternity leave.[46] A woman adopting a baby is entitled to the same paid leave that birth mothers get after the birth.

The stipend, paid by the social security agency, was 84 percent of the mother's base salary up to a maximum of 11,340 francs ($1,742) per month as of 1991. A monthly minimum stipend of 1,253 francs ($192) is available even for those with no current job, provided they had a job immediately before the pregnancy or during it.[47] The *Assurance Maternité* fund also pays all of the medical costs of pregnancy and delivery. Fathers are allowed four days of paid leave, and either parent may request unpaid leave for up to two years after a child's birth or adoption. However, in smaller workplaces, where a council of fellow workers judges the absence to be disruptive, the request may be disallowed.

By comparison, the United States recently adopted the Family and Medical Leave Act, which requires employers to offer unpaid leave to new parents of up to twelve weeks. Previous legislation had required those employers who offer paid sick leave to allow women who give birth to use their regular paid sick leave to cover the period of disability arising from the pregnancy and birth.

Subsidy for Using Licensed Family Day Care:
AIDE À LA FAMILLE POUR L'EMPLOI D'UNE ASSISTANTE
MATERNELLE AGRÉÉE

In France, the government has for years been making an effort to get rid of unregulated care while increasing the availability of good-quality family day care. It has established an official credential for providers it considers adequate, and an official title: *assistante maternelle agréée*. To get this credential, the day-care provider's home must be inspected, and the provider must go through a course of training, get liability insurance, and pass a medical examination, which is repeated annually. Family day-care providers in the United States are much more loosely regulated.

Assistantes maternelles agréées are trained and supervised by the PMI. They can care for up to three infants at a time, their own included. A privately hired *assistante maternelle agréée* negotiates a per-child price with the parents. However, there is an official floor, which has increased from 1,384 francs ($213) per month in 1991 to 3,125 francs ($510) per month as of July 1995, for one child sent on a regular basis.[48] This is far higher than a family day-care provider in the United States would be likely to charge.[49]

The French program that subsidizes licensed family day care is *Aide à la Famille pour L'Emploi d'une Assistante Maternelle Agréée* (AFEAMA). Since 1992, the AFEAMA program has been augmented by a cash payment of 519 francs ($79) per month for parents who place their child with an *assistante maternelle agréée*. The government also creates an incentive to become certified by offering health insurance, unemployment insurance, and credit toward an old-age pension to *assistantes maternelles agréées*. Under the AFEAMA program, the 30.7 percent social security taxes on earnings that the employer normally pays and the 13.45 percent social security tax that the employee normally pays are forgiven. These exemptions create additional financial incentives: the family's cost of hiring a child-care worker is greatly reduced and the wages of privately employed child-care workers are subsidized. This benefit removes the family's and the worker's incentive to keep the employment relation clandestine, something that is relatively easy to do for those who work at home and that is common in the United States.

Subsidies for Nannies: ALLOCATION DE GARDE D'ENFANT À DOMICILE

The *Allocation de Garde d'Enfant à Domicile* (AGED) allowance is available when a nanny is hired to care for a child under three in the family home. To receive this benefit, each member of a couple or the single parent must hold a job. The allowance is designed to reimburse social security taxes on the child-care worker's salary that the family and the child-care worker are legally obligated to pay. In 1991, it allowed payments up to a maximum of 2,000 francs ($307) per month. Reflecting France's desire to relieve the shortage of care for children under three, the maximum was raised to almost

4,000 francs in 1995 for those children, and it was made available to children aged three to six, at a maximum level of almost 2,000 francs per month.

Parent's Child-raising Allowance:
ALLOCATION PARENTALE D'ÉDUCATION

As of 1991, the *Allocation Parentale d'Éducation* (APE) benefit was paid to a parent staying home to take care of a child if the following conditions were met: (1) the family has at least three children, (2) at least one child is under age three, and (3) the parent staying home with the child worked at least two years in the ten years preceding the birth. The benefit in 1991 was 2,716 francs ($417) per month. In the baby's third year, the parent who has gone back to work half-time is entitled to half the monthly stipend. By 1995, this benefit was available to families with two children if the caregiver had two years of paid work in the five years preceding the birth.

This benefit might be considered the "ghost" of the housewife's allowance that was inserted into the family allowance system in 1938. Pronatalist organizations had campaigned for it as a means of increasing the birthrate, as had Catholic women's groups, who argued that anything but a total devotion to maternity on the part of women contravened God's natural law.[50] Ironically, in its present incarnation as the APE, the only mothers who can collect the "housewife's allowance" are those who have demonstrated a commitment to the labor market.

Income Tax Breaks for Child-Care Expenses

Parents paying for child care outside the home to an *assistante maternelle agréée* or to a child-care center are given a deduction from their taxable income of up to 15,000 francs ($2,304) per year.[51] Those employing a child-care worker within the home can reduce their tax liability by half the wages and social security taxes they pay, up to a maximum of 13,000 francs ($1,997). American parents, by contrast, get a maximum child-care credit of $1,440 to offset their taxes.

SUMMARY OF FRENCH CHILD-CARE PROGRAMS

The French child-care program is strongest for children between two-and-a-half and six years of age, where it emphasizes child development. Of the French expenditure in 1991 for child care, 58 percent of the money went into virtually total coverage for out-of-home programs for children two-and-a-half to six years old. The coverage for children under two-and-a-half is far less complete. Based on 1991 costs, the French would have to more than triple expenditures for the under-two-and-a-halfs to achieve total coverage for them, assuming that parents are willing to put those children into out-of-home care. What the French have tried to do instead, however, is to reduce the proportion of children under two-and-a-half who receive unregulated care from a nonrelative.

In the United States, most of the public "child care and development" money goes to half-day Head Start and public kindergarten programs. Much of the federal child-care money goes to care for the children of welfare mothers who are not in jobs, but are receiving job training, some of it of dubious value.[52] American government entities spend on child care and development about half of what programs equivalent to the French ones would require. However, American programs do far less than half of what the French programs do to provide child care that will allow parents to hold jobs.

CHAPTER 4

French Payments to Raise Children's Living Standards

T HE FRENCH GOVERNMENT'S cash and housing benefits are the most expensive components of its program for children's well-being.[1] These programs cost the French government 135.7 billion francs—equivalent to $96.4 billion for the United States—in 1991. An additional 50 billion francs ($36 billion in our terms) are given out as income tax breaks. The benefit levels change each year, along with the minimum wage, and they keep up with cost-of-living changes. Although conservative governments have been elected in recent years, the programs described here are not under significant attack in France, despite the huge expenses they entail.[2] These programs continue to be popular because many of them benefit all families with children, regardless of their income level.

These programs reflect both a concern for the country's children, and the French desire to encourage births. The basic design of the most important programs date from an era when all births, even unplanned births to poor, single mothers, were viewed positively because they provided valuable recruits to the army. (Interestingly, however, the desire for births in recent times has not resulted in policies that limit access to contraception and abortion. Contraception has been legal since 1967 and free of charge to minors since 1974. Abortion in France has been legal since 1975.[3])

Immigration in France, much of it from the African continent, has reduced the country's ethnic homogeneity—and with it has reduced the national enthusiasm for all babies. Immigrants receive almost all benefits, provided their residence in France is legal.[4] Parts of the French electorate would like to see the immigrants repatriated, and regret that they are producing children on French soil. To some, these benefit programs encourage the immigrants' already-high birthrates. Nevertheless, the French benefit programs have retained broad support because they do not narrowly focus on the poor, in which immigrant groups figure disproportionately.

Moreover, as has already been emphasized, realistic people in France know that children of immigrants are likely to stay in the country. If these children grow up in deprived circumstances, they cannot contribute to the well-being of the French nation. On the contrary, keeping groups in a marginalized condition creates crime and dependency problems, degrades urban habitats, and exacerbates political problems.

The ten French benefit programs that will be outlined in this chapter were not designed as a cohesive whole. When the government perceived gaps in existing programs, they added new programs, instead of redesigning the existing programs to produce a simpler set of payout rules. Even French officials consider the structure of their programs to be overly complicated.[5] This complexity is one reason we would not want to copy slavishly the details of the French benefit programs. The pronatalist tilt that sends disproportionately large benefits to families with three or more children and gives relatively little to one-child families would be unlikely to find favor in the United States—particularly if it was thought to increase birth rates in the lower-income groups.

Table 4.1 provides a list of French income supplementation programs for families with children. Slightly more than half of the total expenditure on these programs goes to benefit schemes that are available to families regardless of their income. Most of the remainder goes to programs that benefit both married couples and single parents who have below-average wage incomes. Only about 5 percent of the expenditure goes for the two welfare-like programs narrowly restricted to people with little or no wage income. The contrast with U.S. transfer programs is dramatic and will be explored in the later chapters on the United States.

HOW GOVERNMENT CASH BENEFITS ADD UP

What is the magnitude of the cash benefits that France provides, and how are they distributed among families? Table 4.2 shows the

TABLE 4.1 FRENCH GOVERNMENT EXPENDITURE ON PAYMENTS TO
IMPROVE LIVING STANDARDS OF FAMILIES WITH
CHILDREN, 1991

Payments	Billions of Francs	Billions of Dollars[a]
Available to all families	Fr 75.326	$53.533
Family allowances (AF)	64.497	45.837
New baby allowances (APJE)	5.867	4.170
Child support assurance (ASF)	3.629	2.579
Handicapped child allowances (AES)	1.333	0.947
Available to families with modest or no wage income	56.510	40.161
Housing allowances (ALF + APL[b])	31.737	22.556
Continuation of APJE until age 3	14.086	10.011
Continuation of APJE beyond age 3 for large families (CF)	8.699	6.182
Back-to-school allowances (ARS)	1.986	1.411
Available only to those without substantial wage income	7.192	5.111
Single parent subsistence (API)	3.841	2.730
Minimum income to assist job entry (RMI)	3.351	2.381
Total	139.028	98.806

Sources: Figures for all programs other than RMI come from CAF statistiques; prestations familiales, 1991 (Paris: Caisse Nationale des Allocations Familiales, 1991), 120. Figures for the RMI come from V. Poubelle and B. Simonin, "Le RMI: un million d'allocataires en trois ans," in La société française; données sociales, 1993 (Paris: INSEE n.d.), 548–56.
Note: These data do not include income tax deductions for families with children. Some totals are slightly different from sum of amounts due to rounding.
[a] French expenditure translated into dollars of equivalent purchasing power, and then adjusted to take account of the greater number of children in the United States.
[b] Of the APL funds, 66 percent is allocated as going to families with children. See CAF statistiques; prestations de logement: premiers resultats 91 (Paris: Caisse Nationale des Allocations Familiales, 1991), 141.

types and amounts of benefits families with children of various ages receive. The benefit packages shown in the table are those available to families with a "taxable" income of 70,000 francs per year. Such an income would have the purchasing power of an American before-tax income of approximately $16,200.

A single French mother with two young children and low income would get major aid from four kinds of programs, adding up to $502 a month ($6,024 a year) to supplement her wages, exclusive of the child-care benefit payments described in chapter 3. The benefits—the family allowance, a new baby allowance, housing subsidies, and child support assurance—would provide a 37 percent boost to her pretax income, and an even larger percentage increase in her after-tax income, since none of these benefits is taxable. In addition, her access to health insurance would be assured and financed by the social security system.

For one-child and two-child families, benefits are largest when the youngest child is under three years of age, when child-care needs are most acute. The single mother with two children, who gets $502 monthly in benefits when her children are six months and two-and-a-half years-old, sees those benefits dwindle to $368 when both children are over age three. However, by that time the younger child in a two-child family will be in the free public nursery school and the older child will be in grade school. A service will care for them before and after school, and will drop them off and pick them up from school at low cost to the parent.

The relative paucity of benefits for the one-child family, and the generosity of income-supplementing benefits to the three-child family, especially when the children are beyond three years of age, is also shown in table 4.2. While benefits to the single mother with one child decrease to $145 when the child reaches three years old, a low-income single mother with three children gets increased benefits, which amount to $821 a month when her children get to the teen years.[6]

In France, as table 4.2 shows, a married couple is eligible for benefits that are lower than the single mother's because of the child-support assurance received only by the latter. However, couples still receive substantial benefits, so that they have less incentive than couples in the United States to remain unmarried or to break up in order to qualify for government benefits.

Tables 4.3 and 4.4 show how benefits vary with income level. Here, the wage levels are after-tax proceeds from wages that are once, twice, four times, and ten times the minimum wage. The benefit as a percentage of wage income falls off quite rapidly as income increases, but thanks to the non–income-tested benefits, it does not disappear even at large incomes, for families with more than one child.

THE FRENCH BENEFIT PROGRAMS: ELIGIBILITY AND TYPE OF ASSISTANCE

Family Allowances: ALLOCATIONS FAMILIALES

Allocations Familiales—allowances to families with children—administered by the social security system, are the largest compo-

TABLE 4.2 MAJOR MONTHLY INCOME-SUPPLEMENTING BENEFITS IN FRANCE, BY NUMBER AND AGES OF CHILDREN, 1991

Ages of Children in Family	Family Allowance (AF)	New Baby Allowance (APJE)	Means-Tested Large-Family Allowance (CF)	Housing Allowance (APL)[b]	Child Support Assurance (ASF), Single Parent not Receiving Private Child Support	Total, Single Parent	Total One-Earner Couple
Monthly benefits in francs for families with taxable wage income of 70,000 francs[a]							
One-child families							
1 year	Fr 0	Fr 875	Fr 0	Fr 515	Fr 429	Fr 1,819	Fr 1,390
5 years	0	0	0	515	429	944	515
Two-child families							
6 months, 2½ years	610	875	0	927	858	3,270	2,412
5 and 7 years	610	0	0	927	858	2,395	1,537
Three-child families							
1, 4, and 8 years	1,391	875	0	1,407	1,287	4,960	3,673
9, 12, and 16 years	1,867	0	794	1,407	1,287	5,355	4,068

Monthly benefits expressed in dollars for families with pre-tax wage income of about $16,200[c]

One-child families							
1 year	$0	$134	$0	$79	$66	$279	$214
5 years	0	0	0	79	66	145	79
Two-child families							
6 months, 2½ years	94	134	0	142	132	502	371
5 and 7 years	94	0	0	142	132	368	236
Three-child families							
1, 4, and 8 years	214	134	0	216	198	762	564
9, 12, and 16 years	287	0	122	216	198	823	625

Source: Compiled by the author from information in *Barème social periodique*, No. 13 (Paris: Liaisons Sociales, 30 April 1991).

[a] In France, "taxable income" excludes the worker's portion of social security tax, and an additional deduction of 28 percent.

[b] The dollar figures are somewhat smaller than those that would be implied by table 4.7, where the social security tax added back to get gross income was at French levels, rather than at U.S. levels.

[c] For the dollar "pretax income" corresponding to the "taxable income" of 70,000 francs, the concept of income most familiar in the United States was used. To get it, the 70,000 francs taxable income was converted into dollars of equivalent purchasing power; the 28 percent deduction the French are allowed to take for tax purposes was added on and the employee portion of social security taxes at U.S. rates was added.

TABLE 4.3 FRENCH GOVERNMENT TRANSFER PAYMENTS TO COUPLES
(MARRIED OR UNMARRIED) WITH CHILDREN, BY FAMILY
INCOME, 1990 (FRANCS PER YEAR)

Wage Income[a]	Cash Allowances	Housing Subsidy Under ALF	Total Government Aid	Total Resources
One-child family				
0	[b]	[b]	Fr 43,835	Fr 43,835
51,240	Fr 1,828	Fr 7,030	8,850	60,090
102,480	1,828	0	1,828	104,308
204,960	401	0	401	205,361
512,400	401	0	401	512,801
Two-child family				
0	[b]	[b]	57,156	57,156
51,240	11,573	9,673	21,246	72,486
102,480	11,573	2,603	14,176	116,656
204,960	8,750	0	8,750	213,710
512,400	8,556	0	8,556	520,956
Three-child family				
0	[b]	[b]	68,592	68,592
51,240	32,736	11,964	44,700	95,940
102,480	31,394	5,755	37,149	139,629
204,960	25,460	0	25,460	230,420
512,400	23,061	0	23,061	535,461

Source: Politique familiale et dimension de la famille (Paris: Centre d'Étude des Revenus et
des Coûts, 1992), 29.
[a] Wage incomes represent the take-home pay that would result from year-round work at
once, twice, four times, and ten times the minimum wage.
[b] A one-child family with total resources less than 43,835 francs received aid to bring it up to
that level, including cash and housing subsidies. Families with more children are brought up
to the levels shown in the table. The aid for couples is provided by the RMI program.

nent of French expenditures for children's well-being. In 1991, they
cost 64 billion francs ($46 billion in American terms). They are not
income-tested: poor and well-off families get the identical benefit,
and marital status is irrelevant. The only variable controlling benefits is the number of children. Payment schemes of this type are
common in the countries of Western Europe, as well as in Canada,
Australia, and New Zealand.

In France, the idea that families, particularly large ones, should
get help from the state is an old one.[7] In 1793, the Convention, the
legislative body of the revolutionary period, declared that "the

TABLE 4.4 GOVERNMENT TRANSFER PAYMENTS TO COUPLES (MARRIED
OR UNMARRIED) WITH CHILDREN, BY FAMILY INCOME, 1990
(DOLLARS PER YEAR)

Wage Income[a]	Cash Allowances	Housing Subsidy Under ALF	Total Government Aid	Total Resources
One-child family				
0	[b]	[b]	$6,632	$6,632
7,752	$275	$1,064	1,339	9,091
15,504	277	0	277	15,780
31,008	61	0	61	31,068
77,519	61	0	61	77,580
Two-child family				
0	[b]	[b]	8,647	8,647
7,752	1,751	1,463	3,214	10,966
15,504	1,751	394	2,145	17,648
31,008	1,324	0	1,324	32,331
77,519	1,294	0	1,294	78,813
Three-child family				
0	[b]	[b]	10,377	10,377
7,752	4,952	1,810	6,762	14,514
15,504	4,749	871	5,620	21,124
31,008	3,852	0	3,852	34,859
77,519	3,489	0	3,489	81,008

Note: All the magnitudes in this table are simple purchasing-power equivalents in dollars for 1990 of the amounts expressed in francs in table 4.3.
[a] See note a in table 4.3.
[b] See note b in table 4.3.

fathers and mothers whose only resources are the product of their own toil, have the right to help from the Nation whenever the product of that toil is not in proportion with the needs of their families."[8] The first large-scale implementation of these principles was, however, the result of initiatives by private employers. Family allowances originated in the latter part of the nineteenth century as a voluntary payment by employers to supplement the wages of men who were supporting children.

Many politicians were advocating pronatalist policies at that time, and providing cash help to families with children was seen as a good way to encourage births. Employers may have preferred to keep the control of such schemes in their own hands, rather than relinquish control to the government. By paying benefits limited to men with children, employers were seeking to forestall male work-ers' demands for the payment of a "family wage" to all men. Some employers also saved money by refusing to pay family allowances to working mothers, under the pretext that their children were cov-ered by the legal guardianship of the father.[9] A number of public employers also provided such benefits, and in 1917 they were made mandatory for public employees.

Around the time of World War I, groups of employers who were paying family allowances banded together to set up *caisses de com-pensation*, which collected contributions from employers in propor-tion to the number of their workers, and then made family allowance payments to those employers' workers.[10] Since an employer's pay-ments to the *caisses* did not take account of the number of children its own workers had, employers had no cost incentive to avoid hiring men with children. By 1930, two million workers in over thirty-two thousand companies were covered by these schemes. Civil servants got family allowances from the government. In 1932 a law was passed making the system universal, but leaving large parts of it in private hands; all employers were required to affiliate with a *caisse*. Benefits were made uniform after World War II.

It is the family allowances program, above all others, that reflects the historic pronatalist bent of French policy. Its benefit structure reflects the notion that families with three or more children are the ones making the crucial contribution to maintaining the country's population, and should be supported most heavily. Although the effects of this and other benefit programs on the birthrate have surely disappointed the pronatalists, and the desire to ensure chil-dren's well-being has become more prominent, this structure has been allowed to stand.

A family with only one child gets nothing from this program. The benefit levels for 1991 prescribe 610 francs ($94) a month when a second child is born. For the third and any subsequent children, the family gets an additional 781 francs ($120) for each. When the second child reaches ten years old, the benefit increases by 171 francs ($26) per month. When that child reaches fifteen, the add-on over the basic allowance rises to 305 francs ($47) monthly.[11] A fam-ily with three children ages nine, twelve, and sixteen would get allowances totaling 1,867 francs ($287) a month.

Of the many countries with family allowances, France is the only country with a family allowance structure that provides noth-ing for the first child (see table 4.5).[12] For couples or single mothers

TABLE 4.5 FAMILY ALLOWANCES IN COUNTRIES WHO ARE MEMBERS OF
THE EUROPEAN COMMUNITY, 1990 (IN U.S. DOLLARS)

Country	One Child	Two Children	Three Children	Income-tested
Belgium	$57	$162	$320	no
Denmark	61	122	183	no
Germany	25	92	204	partly
Greece	5	21	57	yes
France	0	91	207	no
Ireland	21	41	61	no
Italy	14	55	117	yes
Luxembourg	46	141	310	no
Netherlands	36	45	48	no
Portugal	9	18	27	partly
Spain[a]	2	4	6	no
United Kingdom	46	92	138	no

Source: Digest of Statistics on Social Protection in Europe. Volume 4: Family (Luxembourg: Office for Official Publications of the European Communities, 1993), 73, converted from *ecus* to dollars of purchasing-power parity.
[a] In 1991, family allowances in Spain were increased twelvefold, and exceeded those of Ireland. However, they became income-tested.

with only one child and a low income, cash benefits are available from other programs, and they get substantial help with child care and housing costs. Single parents in the upper part of the income scale with one child get only child support assurance.

Family allowances go on unconditionally until the child is sixteen. Benefits are paid for children up to age eighteen provided the child earns less than 55 percent of the adult minimum wage—*Salaire Minimum de Croissance* (SMIC). Benefits can go on until age twenty if the child is in school or in an apprenticeship and has limited earnings.

The United States has no program that gives the same benefits to families in all parts of the income scale, and therefore no program comparable to the French family allowances. It does, as France does also, charge lower income taxes to families with children, but these benefits actually increase as family income increases for part of the income range, and those families exempt from income taxes on account of low income do not get them.

New Baby Allowance: ALLOCATION POUR JEUNE ENFANT

When a woman becomes pregnant in France, she is entitled to receive a New Baby Allowance—*Allocation Pour Jeune Enfant*

(APJE)—each month, starting with the third month of pregnancy. In 1991, the payment was 875 francs ($134) per month. All mothers, regardless of income or number of children, receive this payment during pregnancy, and continue to receive it until the child reaches three months of age.

Payments under the New Baby Allowance supplement the family's income at a stressful time and act as a mild incentive to continue a pregnancy. They are also an incentive to mothers to follow a government-set compulsory schedule of free prenatal medical examinations and, after the birth, to bring the baby into a free pediatric clinic or a private doctor for regularly scheduled checkups. Mothers are warned that they may lose their rights to the APJE if they fail to appear for the scheduled appointments.

The result is that in France virtually all pregnant women and young babies get preventive health care, all at government expense. In the United States, by contrast, many poor urban and rural women go through their pregnancies without prenatal care, and they do not seek preventive care for their newborns, because they lack health insurance, because of ignorance or inexperience, or because health facilities are inadequate or nonexistent in their communities.

If a French family has a low-to-modest income, payments under the New Baby Allowance can go on until the youngest child reaches three years of age.[13] The income ceiling that determines a family's eligibility for the extension of the full benefit beyond the baby's third month depends on the number of children, whether the family has one or two earners, and whether the family contains a couple or a single parent living alone.

For a one-earner couple with one child in 1991, the gross income ceiling, exclusive of other government benefits, for the full benefit to continue beyond the third month is 123,421 francs ($18,959).[14] For a two-earner couple or a single parent, the ceiling is 163,106 francs ($25,055). For each additional child the income ceiling rises by 29,621 francs ($4,550) per year. At incomes above these ceilings the benefits are reduced, and become zero when income rises 9,036 francs ($1,388) beyond the ceiling.

Judging by the number of beneficiaries, a high proportion of families with children receive the extended APJE benefits beyond their child's third month. In 1991, 513,000 families were receiving the non-income-tested benefit, and 1,389,000 families were receiving the income-tested extension benefits.[15] Since the former last one year and the latter last 2.75 years, this suggests that more than 98 percent of families with children receive the extended benefits. It is possible that the income ceilings on the extended benefit are not rigorously enforced.

By the time the extended APJE benefits end, almost all children are enrolled in the *école maternelle*. The extended benefits of the APJE can thus help those parents whose children are not accommodated in the public *crèches* with out-of-pocket child-care expenses, and those who lose wages by staying home, until their children can attend a public facility.

Child Support Assurance: ALLOCATION DE SOUTIEN FAMILIAL

In France, as in the United States and all other Western countries, a biological parent who does not live with his or her child has a legal obligation to contribute to its support. The obligation exists whether or not the child's parents were married at the time of birth. However, such legal child support obligations tend to be difficult to establish and to enforce.

The idea of *Allocation de Soutien Familial* (ASF)—Child Support Assurance—is that the government undertakes an obligation to enforce the collection of legally established child support payments, and, that in cases where the government has failed to collect, the custodial parent receives from the government some minimum amount instead. (The United States at present has no such program, although proposals have been made to adopt one.[16]) This principle has been only partially implemented in France; the right to collect a payment from the government if the absent parent does not pay is limited to single parents. The Child Support Assurance benefit in 1991 was 429 francs ($66) per month per child and is not income-tested. As in the case of family allowances, these benefits can go on until the child is twenty, provided he or she is in school.

If the absent parent is dead or has left the country, the remaining parent can draw benefits from this program with no conditions attached. However, if the absent parent is living in France and is capable of making payments, the single parent who wants to receive benefits from the Child Support Assurance program must go through the procedures necessary to establish a legal child-support award, including the establishment of paternity. Of approximately 950,000 female and 159,000 male single parents in France in 1991, 423,000 received this benefit.[17]

When this program was originally established in 1970 its focus was on helping the families in which orphans live, and they are still included as beneficiaries. Widows or widowers raising children also benefit from it. Couples or single persons who adopt children, whether orphaned or not, can also draw benefits from the Child Support Assurance program.

In France, child support awarded by the courts is by no means restricted to the low level guaranteed by the Child Support Assurance program, and government help is available to enforce such higher awards. If child support payments are not made for two months, the parent bringing up the child may assign the government the right to receive the child support payment. When this happens, the government collects from the absent parent, and the custodial parent receives the Child Support Assurance, plus any money over and above the level that the government collects from the absent parent.

Handicapped Child Allowance: ALLOCATION D'ÉDUCATION SPÉCIALE

The *Allocation d'Éducation Spéciale* (AES) is an allowance for families with a handicapped child. In 1991 the amount was 1,982 francs ($304) a month for children who need constant help in the ordinary acts of life (eating, using the toilet, dressing, and so forth) and 1,067 francs ($164) for a child who needs less help. It is not income-tested. This benefit goes to relatively few families and is modest in size, yet it enables the parents of these children to hire at least some part-time help.

Housing Allowances: ALLOCATION DE LOGEMENT FAMILIALE *and* AIDE PERSONNALISÉE AU LOGEMENT

In 1991, the French devoted 31.7 billion francs, or the equivalent of $23.6 billion in a country the size of the United States, to programs that help families with children with their housing costs. In per capita terms, the French housing programs spent more than two-and-a-half times as much assisting families with children as American housing programs spent.[18]

The *Allocation de Logement Familiale* (ALF), which dates from 1948, subsidizes the housing costs of families who rent and who have modest incomes. The dwelling unit must meet official standards of size and good condition. Almost all the benefits of the ALF, which increase with the size of the family and decrease as income increases, go to families with children.[19] Another housing program, *Aide Personnalisée au Logement* (APL), was started in 1977. It subsidizes rents in structures that have been built or reconditioned by private owners with government help. It also helps families to purchase

TABLE 4.6 MONTHLY FRENCH HOUSING SUBSIDIES PROVIDED BY THE
AIDE PERSONNALISÉE AU LOGEMENT (APL), FOR COUPLES OR
SINGLE PARENTS, BY ANNUAL TAXABLE INCOME AND
NUMBER OF CHILDREN, 1991 (IN FRANCS)

Net Taxable Annual Income	One Child	Two Children	Three Children
Fr 0	Fr 2,262	Fr 2,598	Fr 2,929
10,000	2,076	2,417	2,760
20,000	1,896	2,242	2,595
30,000	1,674	2,048	2,434
40,000	1,367	1,790	2,232
50,000	1,066	1,496	1,972
60,000	789	1,200	1,689
70,000	515	927	1,407
80,000	208	655	1,132
90,000	0	367	877
100,000	0	88	618
110,000	0	0	341
120,000	0	0	63

Source: Computed from formula in *Barème social périodique*, No. 13 (30 April 1991): 14–17.
Note: Benefits in the table are for families living in Paris and the surrounding area; somewhat lower benefits are paid in less expensive areas. The French concept of taxable income excludes the employee share of social security taxes and a deduction of 28 percent of the remainder.

units.[20] About two-thirds of the APL funds go to assist families with children. A third housing program benefits mostly single adults.[21]

Of the two housing programs that help families with children, the APL is the more generous and serves more beneficiaries. The schedule of housing benefits that families were eligible to receive in 1991 under the APL program is shown in tables 4.6 and 4.7, by size of family and income. The complicated formula by which the benefits are computed takes account of the number of dependents, the household income, and an allowable rent that depends on location—being higher for Paris and vicinity. Benefits are substantial at very low income levels, but come down rapidly as income increases. A family with a single worker earning the average male salary would not be eligible for a housing allowance unless the family had three or more children.

Means-tested Large-Family Allowance: COMPLÉMENT
FAMILIAL

The *Complément Familial* (CF) program helps lower-income families with three or more children that have lost access to New Baby

TABLE 4.7 MONTHLY FRENCH HOUSING SUBSIDIES PROVIDED BY THE
AIDE PERSONNALISÉE AU LOGEMENT (APL), FOR COUPLES OR
SINGLE PARENTS, BY GROSS ANNUAL INCOME AND NUMBER
OF CHILDREN, 1991 (IN DOLLARS)

Gross Annual Income	One Child	Two Children	Three Children
$0	$347	$399	$450
2,000	324	376	429
4,000	301	354	408
6,000	276	332	387
8,000	243	305	367
10,000	205	270	340
12,000	168	233	307
14,000	132	196	271
16,000	97	160	236
18,000	61	127	200
20,000	24	93	166
22,000	0	56	134
24,000	0	20	101
26,000	0	0	69
28,000	0	0	31

Source: Computed from formula in *Barème social périodique*, No. 13 (Paris: Liaisons Sociales, 30 April 1991), 14–17.
Note: Benefits in the table are for families living in Paris and the surrounding area; somewhat lower benefits are paid in less expensive areas. The incomes and benefits in this table are *not* the dollar equivalents of the magnitudes in table 4.6. The benefit corresponding to the dollar gross income (before any taxes or deductions) was computed by converting gross dollar income into francs, getting the taxable income that would correspond to it in France, figuring the benefit in francs corresponding to that taxable income, and then converting the benefit back to dollars.

Allowance payments because their youngest child is older than three years. The CF benefit is lost if a new baby is born, making the family once again eligible to receive New Baby Allowance payments. To get this benefit, which is a per-family benefit, rather than a per-baby benefit, the family must meet the income-ceiling requirements applicable to the extension of the New Baby Allowance beyond the baby's third month. In 1991, the benefit was 794 francs ($122) per month.

Back-to-School Allowance: ALLOCATION DE
RENTRÉE SCOLAIRE

The *Allocation de Rentrée Scolaire* (ARS) is an annual payment (375 francs in 1991, or $57) made at the start of the school year for each child between six and ten years of age. When a child of fifteen is apprenticed, this allowance may also be claimed. It is only available to families of modest means. Such a benefit does not exist in the United States. A family with one child could claim the allowance if its annual income, exclusive of government allowances, was below 115,028 francs ($17,669) in the previous year. For each additional child, the ceiling is raised by 19,112 francs ($2,936). In 1993, this benefit was quadrupled, supposedly on a temporary basis, and the income ceiling was lowered.

Single-Parent Subsistence Allowance: ALLOCATION DE PARENT ISOLÉ

The *Allocation de Parent Isolé* (API) program gives aid exclusively to single parents, to ensure that the parent's income from wages, child support, and government benefits comes up to a minimum level.[22] The 1991 minimum income level was 2,858 francs ($439) per month for a pregnant woman with no children, and 3,810 francs ($582) for a parent with one child, with 953 francs ($146) per month added for each additional child.

This program, which reaches only those with little or no wage income, has a franc-for-franc reduction in benefits as earnings increase. It is thus the closest French analog to the AFDC program in the United States. However, in the United States, AFDC can support a single mother until her youngest child reaches eighteen years, a period that in principle could last for decades. In France, by contrast, the single-parent subsistence program is a short-term expedient.

The French program's thrust was to give the prospective single parent some breathing space while preparing to enter paid work. The French single parent, in most cases a mother, is eligible to receive API payments as long as she has a child under three. Single parents whose youngest child is over three can also receive payments under the API program, but only for periods that do not exceed twelve consecutive months.[23] By age three most children are toilet-trained and can be placed in a free, government-run nursery school, leaving the single parent free to seek and find paid work.

The structure that the French gave to the Single-Parent Subsistence Allowance, which was instituted in 1977, showed that they expected single mothers to provide a major part of their own and their children's support by holding jobs. Except for very limited transitional periods, French single parents were not given the option American single parents have had, of staying home and caring for their children full-time, with parent and children supported on public funds as long as the youngest child is under eighteen.

However, the rise and persistence of unemployment, which has hit France along with many of the other countries of Western Europe, has forced a softening of that policy. In 1990 France registered a 26 percent unemployment rate for women between twenty and twenty-four, and an 18 percent rate for women aged twenty-five to twenty-nine—rates almost double those for men of those ages.[24]

MINIMUM INCOME TO ASSIST JOB ENTRY: *REVENU MINIMUM D'INSERTION*

The *Revenu Minimum d'Insertion* (RMI) program, instituted in 1988, has allowed many single mothers who exhaust their period of eligibility under API to continue getting benefits, albeit at a reduced rate. API had 131,000 single-parent beneficiaries in 1991, while RMI had 101,000.[25] The RMI program brings the family income of "anybody in difficulty" up to a specified minimum level, depending on family size. To qualify, a person must be above age twenty-five. Noncitizens must have been in the country at least three years, making RMI the only income supplementation program that treats legal immigrants differently from citizens.[26] In theory, the stipend is given on the condition that the person is receiving job training or looking for a job—any activity designed to integrate him or her into the work force. To this end, a formal contract containing a plan of action must be drawn up, signed, and approved by a government functionary. However, a survey done in 1991 showed that more than half of the RMI beneficiaries were without such contracts, and some of those who had them were hazy as to what they called for.[27] The high unemployment rate in France and the rest of Europe, which has made integration of the long-term unemployed so difficult, has taken the starch out of the enforcement of such requirements.

The main clientele of the RMI program are long-term unemployed single people with no children, who constitute about 60 percent of the beneficiaries. However, in 1991, 21 percent of the households benefiting from RMI consisted of single parents and their children, and another 16 percent consisted of couples with children.[28]

The RMI benefit in 1991 brings a single parent with one child up to a monthly income level of 3,219 francs ($494) and a single parent with two up to 3,863 ($593). Couples get 3,863 francs ($593) and 4,507 ($692). For each additional child the income rises by 858 francs ($132). As is the case with the API, the RMI recipient loses a franc for every franc brought into the family by work for pay. Single parents who exhaust their API benefits and switch to the RMI program lose 16 percent of their already-low stipend.[29]

A simple way of gauging the difference between AFDC in the United States and the welfare-type programs (API and RMI) in France is to compare their importance in the income supplementation programs for families with children. In the United States, AFDC has been the largest income supplementation program; in France, API and RMI constitute a far smaller part of the government cash going to families with children. The reason is, of course, that France gives much more in the way of benefits to families with full-time earners than does the United States. The result, as we have seen, is that when people in France get a chance to leave welfare, they see it as a chance to improve their condition, because they will get substantial benefits from nonwelfare programs, which, when added to their wage, will finance a decent standard of living. Americans on welfare have no such outlook.

Social Aid for Children: AIDE SOCIALE À L'ENFANCE

The French distinguish programs that help with common life events—such as having children, short to medium-term unemployment, sickness, and retirement—from those programs that deal with more unusual difficulties including long-term unemployment, special financial problems, severe mental or physical handicap, and cases where child protection is of concern. Programs of the former type are classified as "insurance" (*assurance*), and their benefits are dispensed under fixed rules. The latter type—which includes the RMI program—are classified as "social solidarity" (*solidarité*), and the cash benefits and services they offer are controlled by officials who exercise discretion in their disbursement.[30]

The *Aide Sociale à l'Enfance* (ASE) program is a social solidarity program that spends most of its funds on children in foster homes and in institutions whose parents cannot care for them.[31] Like its American counterparts, which include child protection agencies and foster parent programs, it is carried on by regional and local officials, with the central government paying a share of the expenses. The French program also sends government-employed housekeepers to cook, clean, and perform child care for families in which the parents are under stress. A program of discretionary cash payments is available to families in extraordinarily difficult financial circumstances, although some of the payments formerly made by the ASE program now come out of the RMI program.

(Neither the French nor the American expenditures for social aid programs are included in the tables in this chapter or in the summary statistics in chapter 2, because American expenditures for this function, almost all of which are spent by states and localities, cannot be documented. The French spent 16.5 billion francs (the equivalent of $11.7 billion in the United States) on these activities in 1986.[32])

Reductions in Income Tax Obligations

Both France and the United States allow families with children to pay lower income taxes the more children they have. The French income tax code defines taxable income as family income net of government benefits and social security taxes and net of certain deductions that come to 28 percent of wage income. Taxable income is then divided by a "family size divisor" (*quotient familial*).[33] It is estimated that the use of the family size divisor in 1987 caused a reduction in tax revenues of 47.2 billion francs (which would have been $28.3 billion in a country the size of the United States if the per-child reduction in taxes was the same as in France).[34] The analogous income tax breaks in the United States, which take the form of dollar deductions from taxable income per child, are estimated to have cost the U.S. Treasury $25 billion in 1990.[35] In addition, deductions are allowed for child-care expenses in both countries.

THEIR $134 BILLION VERSUS OUR $90 BILLION

In 1991, the U.S. government spent $90 billion on income supplementation for families with children, including reductions in taxes on income.[36] Those expenditures helped the families that received them but left 21 percent of families with children below the poverty line. In 1991, the French government programs for income supplementation sent 189 billion francs (equivalent to $134 billion in the United States) to families with children, ensuring that all but 5.7 percent of French families with children had sufficient resources to keep them out of poverty.

With the exception of the income tax breaks, which help only families with substantial wage income,[37] the U.S. programs for supplementing the incomes of families with children are grossly unpopular with conservatives, and their anger has found a wide echo in the general population. As of early 1996, the Congress of the United States was engaged in writing bills that reduced such expenditures, that restricted eligibility for them, and that removed the obligation of the government to provide them to all eligible families.

By contrast, these programs have remained popular among the French; even in periods when the electorate has favored conservative politicians, nobody has suggested their abolition. Indeed, they have been extended in recent years, and promises to extend them further were a feature of the presidential election campaign in 1994. The difference is due in part to differences in history, culture, demographics, and political style. But an important part is surely due to differences in program design. Although the French programs are unnecessarily complicated, they do incorporate in their basic structure two sensible ideas that American programs lack— that government assistance works best when it is widely distributed, and that government programs should encourage and reward working at a job.

❖ CHAPTER 5 ❖

Medical Services for Child Well-Being in France

F RANCE, like almost all of the world's high-income countries except the United States, maintains a system of national health insurance that gives all legal residents—and thus all of their children—access to medical care. Since the end of World War II, France has also maintained a special public health service network, the *Protection Maternelle et Infantile* (PMI), whose mission is preventive care for pregnant women and children. It systematically maintains computerized records on virtually every pregnant woman and every new baby in France. It successfully pushes prenatal exams and timely immunizations for all, and actively offers help to families in situations that could jeopardize their physical or mental health. The French public health authorities train and deploy a corps of *puéricultrices*, special nurses with extensive training in the care of infants and the administration of services for young children. The *puéricultrices* serve many functions: visiting the homes of at-risk infants, running neighborhood centers to which parents may bring young children for diagnosis and medical advice, supervising day nurseries for infants, educating and accrediting home day-care providers, and doing educational outreach work to promote child health. Despite its greater coverage and more systematic organization in the medical field, in 1991 France spent 9.1 percent of its gross domestic product on health care, compared with 13.4 percent spent in the United States.[1]

MEDICAL INSURANCE

About 95 percent of France's legal residents are covered by the social security system, which includes health insurance. The remaining 5 percent have access to alternative insurance schemes and to public funds to help them finance payments, if necessary. France thus avoids the situation of the United States where millions of people, many of them children, are uninsured.

Table 5.1 gives an estimate of the French government's expenditure on health care for families with children. Such expenditures are financed by a social security tax on wages of 18.5 percent, of which the employer pays 12.6 percent and the worker pays 5.9 percent. Private-practice physicians who sign up with the system agree to an official schedule of fees.[2] Patients choose their own physicians. Medical care connected to pregnancy and birth is free, and certain

TABLE 5.1 GOVERNMENT SPENDING IN FRANCE FOR MEDICAL CARE
FOR FAMILIES WITH CHILDREN, 1991

Type of Care	Billions of Francs	Billions of Dollars[a]
Public spending for care of ill children[b]	Fr 48.2	$62.5
Public spending for care of ill adults in families with children[b]	71.6	92.9
Medical expenses for maternity	18.9	24.6
PMI	1.7	2.3
Other preventive care for children	3.4	4.4
Total	143.8	186.7

Sources: Total spending for illness and for maternity: *Les comptes de la sécurité sociale, rapport juillet 1992* (Paris: Commission des Comptes de la Sécurité Sociale, 1992), 121, 257. Expenditures on the PMI and other preventive care: *Comptes nationaux de la santé, rapport mai 1992* (Paris: Ministère de la Solidarité, de la Santé et de la Protection Sociale, 1992), 14, table 1. Data on families with children as a share of the total population: *Tableaux de l'économie française, édition 1992* (Paris: Institute National de la Statistique et des Études Économiques, 1992), 26. Data on relative cost of medical care by age: Andrée Mizrahi and Arié Mizrahi, *Debours et depenses medicales selon l'age et le sexe* (Paris: Centre de Recherche d'Étude et de Documentation en Économie de la Santé, March 1985), 73, table 27. Conversion of francs spent on medical care into dollars of equivalent purchasing power based on material in *Health Systems,* volume 2 (Paris: OECD, 1993), 66. Totals may not sum due to rounding.
[a] French expenditure translated into dollars of equivalent purchasing power, and then adjusted to take account of the greater number of children in the United States.
[b] Estimated as a share in the expenditures of the social security system on "illness," based on the share of children and parents in the French population and the relative intensity of use of care by relevant age group.

preventive care for babies is also free. For other medical care, patients pay 30 percent of fees for visits to physicians and stays in hospitals, and the insurance fund pays the rest. Some prescribed drugs are completely reimbursed; others are partially reimbursed. Supplementary insurance covering unreimbursed payments can be obtained privately. Low-income people in financial difficulty receive help with such payments from the discretionary funds of the *Aide Sociale*.

THE INFANT HEALTH MOVEMENT

The establishment in 1945 of the PMI, France's service of protective care for pregnant women and children, was the culmination of a long historical process. Since the mid-1800s, fears of "depopulation" have raised government concern about infant mortality and motivated the establishment of programs to prevent it. Lowering infant mortality rates would, it was hoped, serve as a partial offset to the country's chronically low and falling birthrate. Politicians, forever anxious about the country's ability to sustain an army large enough to hold off the Germans, were wont to count up the number of extra regiments the army might have had if infant mortality had been lower.[3]

One source of concern was the widespread traditional practice in French cities of sending newborns to rural areas to be nursed by peasant women, sometimes with poor results. Regulation and eventual elimination of this practice became an early aim of government health authorities; local statutes regulating wet-nursing date back at least to 1715. In 1873, legislation was passed to create a national system for the regulation and inspection of wet nurses. Under this law, local public health offices were organized, a corps of medical inspectors was established, and a system for collecting medical statistics was begun.[4] The wet-nursing industry was disrupted by the First World War, and the practice died out, but the efforts to regulate it had created a tradition of government expenditure, activism, and, one might say, intrusiveness, on behalf of infant health.

At the beginning of the twentieth century, with women's employment increasing, attention was turned to the harsh conditions under which poor working women gave birth and cared for their infants. In response, companies who employed large numbers of women founded *mutualités maternelles* to provide paid maternity leave for them. These associations in time expanded their activities to provide prenatal care, baby clinics, cash assistance, and, where needed, a home helper for new mothers. Originally financed by employer levies on women workers, the *mutualités* soon obtained government and employer subsidies. In 1912, the French legislature passed a bill that mandated paid maternity leave; monetary benefits were conditional on receiving home visits from the local welfare bureau.[5]

The bloodletting of World War I strengthened the movement for infant health in France. In the United States at that time, activists inside and outside government were also mounting programs promoting infant health. The American Red Cross, which aided France during and just after the war, set up French counterparts to the then-vibrant American visiting-nurse programs and helped finance the first French schools specializing in the training of pediatric nurses.[6] While the American infant health movement withered and died, the French movement continued to gain strength, culminating in the panoply of health care, child care, and income supplementation programs in operation today.

In the decade before World War II, France, for all of its history of official concern with infant health, had higher death rates than many countries with comparable economies, including the United States. In 1945, the year the Germans were driven out of France, infant mortality spiked to an astounding 110 per 1,000 births. As one of its first acts, the new postwar government founded the PMI in November of 1945, just ten months after the liberation.

Table 5.2 shows infant mortality rates in France and the United States from 1945 to 1988. (Some of the drop in French rates since

TABLE 5.2 INFANT MORTALITY IN FRANCE AND THE UNITED STATES, 1945–88 (DEATHS PER 1,000 LIVE BIRTHS)

Year	France	United States		
		White	Black	Total
1945	110.0	36.9	60.3	39.8
1950	52.0	26.8	44.5	29.2
1960	27.4	22.9	43.2	26.0
1970	18.2	17.8	30.9	20.0
1980	10.0	11.0	21.4	12.6
1988	7.8	8.5	17.6	10.0

Sources: Les dossiers de l'obstetrique No. 193, 19° Année (March 1992); U.S. Bureau of the Census, *Statistical Abstract of the United States, 1992* (Washington, 1992); U.S. Bureau of the Census, *Historical Statistics of the United States, Colonial Times to 1970*, part 1 (Washington, 1975).

1945 is the result of improved living conditions on account of higher income.[7]) The French infant mortality rate is considerably lower than the average rate in the United States. In comparing the rates in the two countries, it should be noted that about 12 percent of babies born in France are born to foreign mothers, most from North Africa and sub-Saharan Africa.[8] Infant mortality in these vulnerable groups has not been allowed to rise to the levels afflicting the African American population.

THE SCOPE OF *PROTECTION MATERNELLE ET INFANTILE*

The PMI provides the administrative structure for an aggressive national program of preventive care in the field of maternal and infant health.[9] A team of medical professionals from the United States who visited France recently to study the operations of the PMI, and found much to admire, called it "a public route to private responsibility."[10]

The PMI keeps track of all pregnancies and newborns. Through its neighborhood centers and its system of record-keeping and home visitation, the PMI keeps an eye on situations that are especially risky—medically and otherwise—to pregnant women and to infants, and tries to provide interventions that might prevent a bad outcome. Where the PMI authorities consider a pregnancy to be high-risk, they dispatch a medical professional to make home visits, subject to the woman's consent. Babies considered at risk also receive home visits. The aim is to help mothers cope with their infants in a healthful and loving way, to diagnose problems early, and to see that remedial steps are taken. The PMI is also concerned that all children have the appropriate immunizations.

The operations of the PMI are by no means restricted to the poor. Alain Norvez, commenting on the history and operation of the PMI, speaks of the ordinance that set the agency up as marking "a change in emphasis from the notion of assistance to that of protection. It was not anymore a matter of carrying help only to disfavored groups in the population, but rather of protecting the entire population. It was not a question of charitable acts, but of the duty of the nation toward its children and itself."[11] Well-off women who have nonroutine pregnancies or have babies with medical problems receive home visits from PMI professionals. However, people from lower-income groups, single mothers, and the immigrant community tend to be disproportionately in need of PMI help, and a high proportion of the agency's resources go to provide services to them. The agency has undertaken an explicit mission to reduce the effect of inequality of income and status on children. When it was starting out, the PMI focused on issues relating to physical health. However, it has widened that focus to include psychological and social concerns, where they relate to the well-being of children.

The management of the PMI has recently been decentralized and each of the ninety-five *départements* into which France is divided has its own organization. However, the national government sets standards for the ratio of medical personnel to births that each branch is supposed to maintain.

The top managers of the PMI apparatus in each *département* are medical doctors. Gynecologists and pediatricians are on the staff on a full- or part-time basis to give consultations to pregnant women and mothers in its neighborhood centers. A large corps of adjunct physicians give vaccinations. A physician supervises the PMI's service for the diagnosis and possible placement of handicapped children, and for the recruitment of appropriate medical, social, and financial aid for the family if the handicapped child is to remain at home. A medical doctor specializing in pediatrics supervises the sanitary conditions of the district's infant nurseries (*crèches*), each of which have a *puéricultrice* (pediatric nurse) in charge. Another physician supervises the regulation and education of the *assistantes maternelles* in the district, women who provide licensed day care in their own homes and who are subsidized by the state. The bulk of the PMI staff consists of the *sages-femmes* (midwives), who do the prenatal home visiting, and *puéricultrices*, who do the postnatal visiting. In addition, the regional PMI is likely to have aboard some child psychologists and someone specializing in the psychomotor problems of infants. The PMI also runs family planning clinics, which give contraceptive and abortion services, and provide marriage counseling. A considerable number of social workers, paid and provided by social service agencies, work with the PMI.

France spent 1.7 billion francs on the PMI budget in 1991, and another 3.4 billion francs for in-school medical examinations, vaccinations, and record-keeping directed at tracking the health problems of babies and children. In the United States, this expenditure would translate to a total of $6.7 billion a year for preventive care for children.

Regional Operations

The scale and scope of the PMI's operations can be gauged from the activities of the local PMI organization that serves the Rhône department, whose main city is Lyon[12] (see table 5.3). It operates in 180 civic centers, maintains 11 centers for family planning and education, and maintains liaisons in all of the hospitals in which women give birth.

TABLE 5.3 OPERATIONS OF THE RHÔNE *PROTECTION MATERNELLE ET INFANTILE*

Variable	Number
Personnel in 1992 (full-time equivalents)	
Physicians on staff	39.4
Midwives (*sages-femmes*)	15
Pediatric nurses (*puéricultrices*)	148
Pharmacist	0.5
Psychologist	1
Marriage counselors	8
Social workers	12
Secretaries	8
Family planning personnel	42
Vital statistics, 1991	
Population	1,509,000
Births	22,613
Pregnancies at risk (%)	10%
Infant mortality (per 1,000 births)	8.9
Rate of prematurity (%)	4.8%
Abortions	7,000
Diagnostic exams for four-year-olds in public nursery schools, 1991	
Children seen	16,422
% population seen	85%
Problems discovered:	
Visual	1,439
Hearing	801
Dental	703
Speech	432
Behavior	329
Other	823
Children sent to specialists (%)	25.4%

Source: Premiers éléments statistiques: PMI 1992. (Lyon: Conseil Général du Rhône, 1993).

The Rhône PMI (officially called the *Protection Maternelle et Infantile et des Vaccinations*) covers an area that had 22,613 births in 1991. The department's infant mortality rate is 8.9 per 1,000—which, as the Rhône PMI annual report points out, is by no means as good as the 4.9 rate achieved by Sweden. The Rhône PMI classes about 10 percent of its pregnancies as risky and actively follows their course. In 1991, the agency followed 726 pregnant women who were judged to have medical problems. It also followed 808 women who had declared their pregnancies late, and took in charge about 700 pregnancies judged to be at "social risk." Thus, the Rhône PMI's fifteen *sages-femmes* each saw about 150 women in the course of that year, and 160 *puéricultrices* made 12,499 visits to newborns.[13]

The Rhône PMI each year gives complete medical exams to all the four-year-olds attending nursery school. In 1992, one in four of these children were found to have a medical problem that needed attention and were referred for care. The service provided 24,200 children under age four with medical consultations; it gave 26,700 vaccination injections to children.

The Rhône PMI's centers for family planning and education gave 19,050 medical consultations, mostly to people under the age of twenty-five, and its marriage counselors participated in 19,766 consultations. The 1992 annual report lists a number of major problems that need further attention: high rates of abortion (with seven thousand performed in 1992),[14] sexually transmitted diseases, and AIDS, which is on the rise.

The budget of the Rhône PMI is listed in its official documents as 13 million francs in 1993, which translates into $3.64 million in dollars of U.S. medical purchasing power.[15] Since 273 people are listed on the staff, this works out to an average cost of $13,333 per employee, suggesting that some of the employees listed are part-time or charged to other budgets.

Medical Care in Pregnancy

The PMI provides a carefully thought-out, step-by-step, centrally controlled system for registering pregnant women and encouraging them to follow all of the PMI's recommended medical procedures. Ideally, prenatal care should begin early, before a woman and her fetus have suffered irreversible damage. The PMI has been extremely successful in getting such care initiated early: only 4 percent of women giving birth in France did not receive care in the first fifteen weeks of their pregnancy. The corresponding figure in the United States was 21 percent.[16]

When a woman residing in France—rich or poor, native-born or immigrant, lawyer or cleaning lady—finds out she is pregnant and decides that she wishes to continue her pregnancy to term, an elaborate PMI program swings into action. In France, no financial barriers exist to deter women from seeking care, as in the United States. On the contrary, the government provides financial incentives to follow a prescribed schedule of seven obligatory prenatal medical exams for each woman, all free of charge. French women can receive a substantial monthly government pregnancy benefit (*L'Allocation au Jeune Enfant*, "Young Baby Allowance") by visiting a doctor and applying for it. They know that delaying that visit beyond the first trimester, and therefore delaying the application for the benefit, could cost them money. If a woman who has registered her pregnancy does not have these exams in a timely manner, her name appears on a computer-generated list, and PMI personnel make efforts to contact her, help her with whatever problems she has, and get her back on track. If she is recalcitrant, she may be threatened with discontinuance of the Young Baby Allowance.

The application form takes less than five minutes to fill out. However, it is artfully devised to elicit information that the PMI will use to track the pregnancy and decide whether it is risky. In addition to supplying her name and address, the woman gives her place and date of birth, the number of children she is already taking care of, the number of previous pregnancies she has had, her usual occupation, whether she currently has a job, and the name of her legal husband, if she has one.

A separate set of questions asks for the name, occupation, and job status of a man, who is referred to only as "*Monsieur.*" The nature of *Monsieur's* relationship to the woman and to her baby is delicately left unspecified, and the form subtly makes it clear that he need not be a husband. Whoever he is, information about him helps in assessing the current economic condition of the household, and may help with future paternity establishment and child-support claims as well.

PMI rules require that babies get nine medical examinations in their first year, three in their second, and eight between their third and sixth birthdays, all at stated intervals, all free of charge. The results of the required examinations of the baby at eight days, nine months, and twenty-four months are reported to the PMI, where they are computerized and used for follow-up and epidemiological research. The exams may be done by a private physician or at the PMI neighborhood center.

Home Visits to Pregnant Women

The vast majority (96 percent) of pregnancies are registered with the PMI during the first trimester. Pregnant women who especially need to be monitored receive regular visits from PMI staff. Women under sixteen years old, those who are having a first baby after the age of thirty-five, those who live apart from other adults, those who are already taking care of three or more children, and those who have had three or more pregnancies are considered to be at risk. The PMI also considers the unemployment of any household member to be a risk factor.[17]

In addition, physicians and hospitals will ask the PMI to schedule visits to women who have high blood pressure, diabetes, heart problems, AIDS, uterine malformation, or any other condition that might lead to premature birth or otherwise threaten the health of the mother or fetus. Women whose previous pregnancies resulted in premature delivery, or a baby with low birth weight, or a malformed or stillborn baby are also marked for visits, as are women expecting multiple births. The government's social services agencies will refer women who have alcohol or drug problems or who live in households where there is a history of violence. Some women make self-initiated visits to the neighborhood PMI centers because they feel they have problems, and they are likely to be put on the list for home visits.[18]

Each prenatal visit includes a medical examination. However, much of what the *sages-femmes* do on these visits is not medical in the strict sense—they give advice about family matters, about problems with older children, and about other government benefits and services. They play the part, perhaps, of a solicitous older sister. In the words of one *sage-femme*, "[O]ne tries to give information, to educate, to reassure, to give advice that has as its purpose helping the woman to achieve an attitude of adult responsibility, and to render her more conscious of the role she has to play in the protection of her own health and that of the child she will have."[19] The major benefits of these visits may be educational and moralebuilding, rather than medical. A recent epidemiological study, for instance, has found that, for French women threatened with pre-mature labor, home visiting does not appear to reduce hospital stays or lead to a better outcome.[20]

Since each *sage-femme* is part of a team that includes doctors, nurses specializing in infant care, psychologists, and social workers, she can recruit help in difficult cases. Much of the *sages-femmes'* work is with women who are poor, isolated, or troubled, but they also visit many better-off women. Thus, receiving such visits is not stigmatizing.

The CARNET DE SANTÉ MATERNITÉ

On a pregnant woman's first medical visit, she is presented with a *carnet de santé maternité*, or "maternal health notebook," put out by the PMI, durably bound in a waterproof cover.[21] She is asked to keep it handy throughout the pregnancy, to bring it to each medical appointment, to bring it to the hospital for the birth, and to save it for reference in future pregnancies. It thus helps maintain continuity in treatment. It has spaces for physicians to record medical information that the PMI deems important, and thus serves as a tactful reminder to private physicians of the PMI's recommended practices. The *carnet* also contains a page to enter the dates of the seven required prenatal visits (the first before the end of the first trimester, and then monthly), and a reminder that a monthly visit must be made before a particular date if the client is to receive the Young Baby Allowance for that month. It notes that two ultrasound examinations should be done. It strongly suggests that if the mother is thirty-eight or older, the fetus should be tested for Down's syndrome and other chromosomal abnormalities.

The *carnet* contains a lot of good advice and useful information, attractively presented with colorful illustrations. It tells the woman to avoid any medicine not prescribed by her doctor, to avoid alcohol and tobacco, and to exercise moderately but to avoid heavy work, and to seek help from her husband, friends, older children, and when she is tired. It mentions that government-supplied household help is a possibility in some cases. The *carnet* reviews what will happen in each month of the pregnancy; for the ninth month, the page shows a picture of a baby emerging from a cabbage (the French equivalent of the stork story), plus a list of the symptoms that indicate she should go to the hospital or maternity center.

A section of the *carnet* is devoted to the new mother's rights and benefits. It tells her about regular government financial benefits and suggests that if she is in a particularly difficult situation she can get additional benefits. She is informed that no employer may use the pregnancy as a reason to refuse to hire or dismiss her. The *carnet* advises her to tell the associated physician at her workplace that she is pregnant. The workplace physician is supposed to see that she is shifted to easier duties, if that is indicated. As noted earlier, an employer does not have the right to require work in the two weeks before the birth and six weeks after it, and if a woman takes that leave she is reimbursed through the social security system. An additional unpaid parental leave is available both to the mother and the father for a year, and the mother has the right to work part-time for as long as three years after a birth or an adoption.

Surveillance of Newborns

The *puéricultrices* who run the PMI service of home visitation of infants maintain a liaison with physicians and social workers at all the hospitals and maternity centers where babies are born. These professionals regularly compile lists of babies who would benefit from home visits after they leave the hospital. Other babies are put on the list to be visited when the obligatory examination at eight days after birth indicates a need. The PMI office examines the physicians' detailed reports to identify babies that would benefit from visits, and sends their names and addresses to the group of *puéricultrices* based in the baby's neighborhood. In addition, some mothers request home visits, in response to letters they receive from the PMI telling them about the possibility of such visits, and listing the various ways in which the *puéricultrice* can help. Sometimes a *sage-femme* who has been visiting a pregnant woman judges that postnatal visits will be needed, and brings along a *puéricultrice* on one of her visits toward the end of the pregnancy to introduce her.[22]

A baby is slated for home visits if the mother is having trouble nursing, is inexperienced, is living in isolation, or shows great anxiety, or if the infant is premature, of low birth weight, or otherwise ill or abnormal. Other indications for home visits include "social problems": families that are not well integrated into the community, that are poor, that have drug or alcohol problems, or that have problems with family violence. Promiscuity on the part of the mother, uncleanliness in the home, or bad housing can also trigger visits. Visits are given to new babies whose older siblings have been poorly cared for or have been repeatedly hospitalized. Babies coming home from foster care or a hospital also receive follow-up home visits.[23]

Babies of immigrants (including the babies of illegal immigrants) get a disproportionate share of visits. Immigrant families are more likely to exhibit the factors that occasion such visits, because of their poverty, language problems, inexperience with French ways and institutions, labor market difficulties, and the strains connected with their special legal status. Mothers from North Africa and sub-Saharan African countries, where most of the immigrants originate, are likely to encounter attitudes in their extended family that are at odds with freedom that women have in modern French society. This may lead to explosive situations that bring a threat of violence both to the mother and the children.

A training manual for *puéricultrices* speaks of the purpose of home visits as "accompanying the mother in her apprenticeship in care of the newborn": helping her to acquire a certain ease in changing and dressing the baby, in holding and feeding it; helping the mother to perceive the signs of hunger, sleepiness, or sickness; helping the mother to recognize and pay attention to the baby's moments of satisfaction, and so helping to establish affectionate ties between the infant and its parents; and helping the mother learn to deal with the baby's fevers, digestive problems, rashes, and so forth.[24] The *puéricultrice* informs the mother about financial aid and social services that are available. In families with many older children or special difficulties, she informs the mother that a government-provided household helper may be available for a time after the baby comes home.

The *puéricultrice* is trained to watch for signs of postpartum depression and for problems the mother might have in dealing with the infant's crying. If the mother's psychological state appears to be deteriorating, the *puéricultrice* alerts a physician.[25] The home visits go on until the mother has adjusted, the baby appears to be developing well, the family is making use of medical care as appropriate, and no signs of mistreatment or other problems are evident. In most PMI branches, a physician must sign an order to cease the visits.

In its first years, the PMI used social workers *(assistantes sociales)* to do all of the home visits. As now, the primary function of the visitor was to help and advise the parents. However, where they judged the child's health or well-being was seriously threatened, the social workers would start proceedings to take the child out of the home. As a result, clients had difficulty viewing these home visits as relaxed, friendly, and unthreatening. The PMI was sensitive to this problem, and in the 1960s and 1970s, medically trained midwives and pediatric nurses replaced the social workers in routine home visitation. The midwives and nurses are better equipped to handle specific medical and behavioral problems, and they come across as helpers and advisers rather than censorious observers.

The social workers still play a part in the agency, and can be called in when serious problems are detected. Of course, children are still removed from homes judged to be dangerous, but that is a rare occurrence. The social workers and the potential threat they pose to parents' autonomy are now far less salient in the agency's operation, and most parents do not have contact with them.

Immunizations and the CARNET DE SANTÉ

For each new baby, the parents receive a *carnet de santé*, which is the baby's counterpart to the pregnant woman's *carnet de santé maternité*. Like the latter, it serves as a record of medical information and treatment, and is brought to all medical exams, so each new physician can see the child's whole medical record. Among the items it records are the contagious diseases the child has had, its hospitalizations, x-rays, allergies, and chronic conditions. The last two pages of the *carnet de santé* distributed by the Rhône PMI are cartoons directed to the parents—one about keeping medicines and dangerous products out of the reach of children, and the other a warning that excessive television watching will impair their child's schoolwork.

The *carnet de santé* has a section where physicians attest with their signature the immunizations they have given the child. Three types are legally required: diphtheria/tetanus, polio, and tuberculosis. Inoculation against measles, whooping cough, rubella, and mumps is recommended by the time the baby is one year old. Children who have not had the required or recommended vaccinations can be brought up to date on their shots when they go to the PMI neighborhood center, at no charge to the parents.

The *carnet* comes with the forms for registering with the PMI the results of the child's three obligatory medical exams. Analysis of the results of the third certificate, due at twenty-four months, shows that ninety-five percent of the children have had or started their immunizations against diphtheria/tetanus, polio, and whooping cough, and that 76 percent have been protected against tuberculosis.[26]

Detection of Child Abuse

Children in France are far more in the eye of the public health authorities than they are in the United States. In addition to receiving home visits and enrolling their young children in the *écoles maternelles*, all French citizens are legally required to report to the authorities any abuse or privation of a child under the age of fifteen. Anyone who observes abuse and fails to report it can be subject to a prison term of up to three years. Medical personnel are officially reminded from time to time that they are subject to such penalties.

The PMI defines maltreatment quite broadly to include not only physical brutality, but also neglect and serious emotional deprivation. Among the warning signs that *puéricultrices* are told to look for in infants and children are sadness, fear, or apathy, baldness on the back of the head, possibly indicating that the infant is not being picked up, and bottles wedged into the baby's bed so it can feed itself.

Puéricultrices making home visits are taught to be alert for abuse where the family is plagued by alcoholism, drug addiction, mental illness, unemployment, or family quarrels. While poverty is a recognized risk factor, abuse—both physical and psychological—is understood to occur at all levels of society. Certain periods that are difficult for the family are of particular concern: when the new baby comes home for the first time, or when an infant who has been hospitalized is brought home.

The professionals recognize the tension between prompt action to protect children who are in danger and preventing false accusations. They find it useful to distinguish among "worry or fear" that abuse could take place, "suspicion" that it might be taking place, and "identifying" that it is taking place.[27] They speak of "signs of risk" and "signs of danger," the latter being more clearly indicative.

The *puéricultrice*'s home visits and her attempts at education and advice constitute the first line of defense for very young children. If this does not take care of the problem, she formally signals to the authorities that an "administrative prevention process," which is relatively nonstigmatizing, should be started. At this "risk" stage, a team of specialists is assigned to work with the family: social workers with special training in abuse, specialized teachers, and perhaps a household worker to help with cooking, cleaning, and child care. A psychologist or psychiatrist is available to consult with the team and to hold sessions with the family. The team can deal with money problems or housing problems by informing the family about the regular benefit programs that are available, and by requesting that the family be given access to special discretionary funds. While all this is going on, the child remains with its family.

More extreme or advanced cases, in which the child appears to be in immediate danger or is already gravely compromised, are reported to the judicial system. If it is decided that the child should, for the present, be kept with its parents, the court may order a program of surveillance and education. Or, the judge may remove the child on a provisional basis to the home of another family member, to foster care, or to an institution. More permanent removal requires a more elaborate judicial procedure.

The French system, elaborate as it is, is not foolproof. Abuse, sometimes fatal, does occur.[28] The natural reticence to report suspicions and the reluctance to take children away from their families does result in some tragic errors, as occur under any system. However, the situation in France must be compared with that in the United States, where children up to the age of six can be completely invisible to the authorities until the hour they arrive in the hospital dead or gravely wounded.

COMPARING FRANCE WITH THE UNITED STATES

In the United States a movement to improve infant health blossomed during the Progressive era at the beginning of the twentieth century. By 1927, however, a modest federal program for infant health in the United States had succumbed to opposition from the private physicians who controlled the American Medical Association, who feared competition from government-sponsored medical programs.[29] By contrast, French physicians have tended to take a positive attitude toward government activism in infant health, and many of them took positions in the bureaucracy that administered such programs. Considerations of family privacy, self-sufficiency, and freedom from government intervention, so prominent on the American scene, have typically not inhibited French government inspections or interventions.

The intensely privatized nature of American health-care delivery for the nonelderly, middle-to-upper-income segment of the population, and the uncoordinated system of individually operating fee-for-service physicians, has translated into a lack of proper care for many pregnant women and young children. Many poor women are too overworked or depressed to get early and regular prenatal care. As noted earlier, in the United States 21.2 percent of women who had live births started prenatal care late (after the fifteenth week of pregnancy), a startling contrast to France's 4 percent.[30] This discrepancy can very likely be explained by the difference in the degree of government intervention in pregnancy in the two countries. In the United States, a pregnant woman who lacks health insurance is on her own to finance and arrange medical care during pregnancy and birth. Some areas have free or low-cost clinics, but some women may not be able to reach them, or they may not have the time for the long wait for service, especially if they have a job. Family members of a pregnant woman may try to motivate and support her in getting appropriate care, but their influence and attention may be limited.

The United States has no system in place to guarantee that a pregnant woman will arrange for timely medical care and show up for medical appointments. No individual physician or clinic has any mandate, incentive, or resources to follow up with pregnant women who are not taking care of themselves.

The uncoordinated nature of the American system of health care and the lack of universal health insurance coverage also make it difficult to deliver and monitor children's immunizations. Only 37 percent of American children aged six months to two years have all of the medically recommended immunizations.[31] Government action toward getting all children immunized has bipartisan support. However, the difficulties in accomplishing such a goal in the United States are illustrated by the fate of President Clinton's attempts to do so.[32] Under Clinton's plan, the government would buy the vaccine at discount prices from the drug manufacturers and distribute it free to physicians. Doctors participating in the program would be required to ask parents if they meet certain low-income criteria and would deliver the vaccine free to eligible children.

It turned out that Clinton's plan could not provide a simple way to get all children immunized at government expense. The aspects of the plan that would inhibit universal coverage included: (1) possible high doctors' charges for administration of the vaccine, (2) lack of a universal system to keep track of children's immunization records and to encourage parents to get their children immunized, (3) threats by the vaccine manufacturers (drug companies) to raise prices on batches sold privately outside the program and to cease research on new vaccines, (4) the drug companies' possible refusal to supply the quantity of vaccine the government would wish to buy, (5) the program's income-eligibility criteria, which excluded many children from the program who might then go unvaccinated, and (6) the likelihood that many doctors would not sign up for the program. Attempts to implement President Clinton's immunization plan, flawed as it was, failed when the distribution of vaccines from government warehouses fell into disarray. The plan was eventually abandoned, a sad monument to American disorganization in matters of children's health.[33]

Had it worked, President Clinton's proposed overall reform of the American system of health-care delivery would have increased access to health care among underserved sectors of the American public. It would have brought universal coverage, an increase in the proportion of the population in health maintenance organizations, and the inclusion of preventive care in everyone's basic health-care package. These developments would have increased the usage of prenatal care and the proportion of children receiving immunizations and checkups.

However, certain essential elements of the PMI operation would have been missing from the envisaged reform, and would have needed separate development. These elements include registration of all pregnancies and births with a medical provider, selection of risky cases, surveillance of such cases, and aggressive attempts to help in the cases deemed to need it. Another essential element would be special government cash benefits to pregnant women and new mothers who follow the prescribed medical regimen.

A very few states in the United States have programs that identify at-risk infants and try to assure that they receive the services they need. In the state of Washington, under a High Priority Infant Tracking Program, the nursing, medical, and social services personnel of community hospitals and perinatal centers are encouraged to identify infants at risk for poor health or poor developmental out-comes. With the permission of the parents and the primary care provider, the infant is registered in the program. Every six months the baby's doctor or clinic receives a questionnaire asking whether the child has been seen and how the child is doing. If the child has not been brought in, a local social service agency makes an attempt to contact the family through letters, phone calls, and home visits, with the purpose of reconnecting the child with medical care. If there are barriers to medical care access, the agency tries to resolve them. Similar programs are in operation in Iowa and North Carolina.[34] The existence of these programs shows that PMI-type operations can be compatible with American traditions. However, the sparsity of such programs means that the United States has thus far not been vigorous in developing them.

The record of child neglect and the high cost of remedial care for premature babies and unimmunized children in the United States has been well publicized, as has the high incidence of outright child abuse. That knowledge may eventually erode the American public's antipathy to government intrusion on private decisions and to putting government pressure on private citizens to "do the right thing," at least where children are concerned. However, an American PMI, if it were to come, would have to come on the crest of a movement for the improvement of child well-being, a movement whose start is hardly in sight.

PART III

American Programs for Children, Past and Future

❖ CHAPTER 6 ❖

American Programs for Children: Keeping Millions Deprived

A S WE HAVE SEEN, American programs designed to aid families with children cost $146 billion of public money in 1991, exclusive of spending for schooling in grades one through twelve. The high incidence of poverty among American children testifies to the inadequacy of these programs and their flawed design. They have been ripe for reform for decades, but despite the tinkering that has been attempted since the late 1960s, their basic structure has been only slightly modified. The most recent idea of conservatives in Congress was to decentralize control of these programs, reduce federal expenditure on them in real terms, reduce the amounts the federal government has required the states to spend on them, and relax the requirement that states offer benefits to all of the eligible, thus ending the "entitlement" of eligible children. Although such changes have been billed as a "reform" or even a "revolution," they would leave intact the basic structure of our existing programs and leave undisturbed their major flaws.

One way to understand the general outlines of American policy, and to understand how that policy will continue to fail our children unless its basic structure is changed, is to think of families with children as divided into three groups. Each group is helped by a distinct set of programs that does little or nothing to help the other two, a major distinction from the more universal types of coverage offered by the French programs. The bottom group contains families that have $10,000 or less in annual wages and accounts for about 13 percent of families with children. Few of the families in this group have an adult with a full-time job. The second group, which comprises another 13 percent or so of families with children, consists of families with at least one adult who has a full-time job, but who receive less than $20,000 in wage income annually.[1] Many of these families are the "working poor," and they lead insecure and difficult lives. The third group consists of families whose wages total more than $20,000 a year.

The American programs and the amounts spent on them are listed in table 6.1. In most of these programs, the benefits are heavily concentrated on only one of the three groups. The main programs helping the bottom group are Aid to Families with Dependent Children (AFDC), Medicaid, food stamps, and the various housing assistance programs. Together, these bottom-group programs cost $96 billion in 1991 and gave little or no help to families in the second group and none to those in the third. The main program for the second group is the Earned Income Tax Credit, for which $9 billion was spent in 1991, which gives little or no help to people in the first and third group. The major benefit to the third group of families comes through state and federal income tax breaks, which cost $25 billion in 1991. The second group gets a minor share of this, and the bottom group gets virtually nothing.

The only substantial government program listed in table 6.1 that benefits all three groups is public kindergarten, listed under "child care and development." Where available on a full-time basis, together with after-school care, kindergarten can perform the same child-minding function as the école maternelle. However, this child-minding help is restricted to one year out of the six pre-elementary years, and for all practical purposes nonexistent in those localities that offer kindergarten only on a half-time basis.

The bottom-group programs keep non–job-holding single mothers and their children from homelessness and starvation. They provide the family with health insurance and enable mothers to care for their children at home. But the benefits are not sufficient to provide a minimally decent standard of living. Many families in the second group live at a standard that is little better, despite the fact that adults in the second group do much more work for pay. Their jobs—laborer, office cleaner, low-level food or hospital worker—

TABLE 6.1 EXPENDITURE FOR GOVERNMENT PROGRAMS FOR CHILDREN IN THE UNITED STATES, 1991

Government Program	Billions of Dollars
Child care and development	$23.9
Head Start	2.4
Public kindergarten[a]	15.0
Federal tax credit for child-care expenses[b]	2.3
Child care and development block grants	0.7
Title XX grants to states used for child-care subsidies	2.0
Child care to avert AFDC	0.8
Child-care food program	0.5
Foster grandparents	0.1
Income supplements	89.9
AFDC	23.0
Social security for surviving children and caregiving parents[c]	2.6
School lunch programs	3.5
Food stamps[d]	12.4
Other feeding programs	3.8
JOBS program	0.9
Housing assistance[e]	8.5
Income exemption for children	
Federal taxes[f]	21.0
State taxes[g]	4.4
Earned Income Tax Credit[b]	9.4
Medical care	32.1
Medicaid to families on AFDC[h]	31.5
Maternal and child health services	0.6
Total	145.9

Source: Where not otherwise indicated, the source is Vee Burke, "Cash and Noncash Benefits for Persons With Limited Income: Eligibility Rules, Recipient and Expenditure Data, FY 1990–92," 93-382 EPW (Washington: Congressional Research Service, 1993).
Note: Data are for the calendar year ending September 30, 1991, except where indicated. Entries may not add to totals due to rounding.
[a] Derived from material in National Center for Education Statistics, *Digest of Education Statistics, 1993* (Washington, 1993).
[b] U.S. Department of the Treasury, *Statistics of Income Bulletin* 12 (Spring 1993): 12.
[c] Estimated from material in *Annual Statistical Supplement to the Social Security Bulletin, 1992* (Washington: U.S. Department of Health and Human Services, 1993).
[d] The attribution of food stamp benefits to families with children is based on the ratio of AFDC recipients to food stamp recipients, and on the ratio of child recipients of food aid to child recipients of means-tested cash benefits. For the latter, see U.S. Bureau of the Census, *Poverty in the United States, 1992,* Current Population Reports, Series P60-185 (Washington: U.S. Government Printing Office, 1993), xviii.
[e] The proportion of households with children among all beneficiaries of housing programs was 45 percent, which is taken to be the share of such households in housing benefits. See *Characteristics of HUD-Assisted Renters and Their Units in 1989* (Washington: U.S. Department of Housing and Urban Development, March 1992).
[f] Estimate for 1990 from C. Eugene Steuerle and Jason Juffras, "A $1000 Tax Credit for Every Child: A Base of Reform for the Nation's Tax, Welfare, and Health Systems" (Washington: Urban Institute, April 1991), 16a.
[g] Estimated by the author, using state income taxes as a proportion of federal taxes.
[h] U.S. Bureau of the Census, *Statistical Abstract of the United States, 1993* (Washington, 1993), 113, 115.

are arduous, dirty, boring, dead-end, and insecure. Many of their employers do not provide free or subsidized health insurance, which most of the members of the lowest group get from the government, and most in the third group get from employers. Thus, the second group's needs for cash are greater than the bottom group's, because many of them need to lay out their own money for health care and for the expenses associated with job holding, such as transportation and child care. On a per capita basis, the second group gets less than 10 percent of what the bottom group gets from the government (see table 6.1).

Life in the second group is so difficult and so precarious that people in the bottom group have little incentive to "move up." A family in the bottom group can truly raise its standard of living only by leaping over the second group and entering the third. That is possible if the parent has been to college and can get a job with adequate wages. It is also possible if the parent is a white man, even without higher education, because he has a better chance at a higher-paying crafts job, with on-the-job training. But in the U.S. labor market, with race and sex discrimination still common, the chance at a well-paying job for black men and for women of all races and ethnic groups without higher education is far lower.[2] For many such people—who predominate among the parents in the first and second groups—making that leap into the third group is improbable. That is why many members of the first group tend either to stay there or go back and forth between the first and the second groups, remaining mired in poverty. Their unhappy choice is between a poverty-stricken life on welfare, but with child-care and medical-care worries at bay, and a poverty-stricken life on an unstable, low-wage job, without substantial government benefits and without assistance for child care and medical bills.

The great defect of American policy toward families with children is the scant help given to the second group, to which the labor market consigns most job-holding mothers without higher education. The problem is well illustrated by a statement of Republican Senator Phil Gramm:

> I'm not going to be swayed by people who want to accuse me of being anti-poor. I'm not going to be swayed by people who say, "You have no compassion." I have great compassion. I think of the unwed mother who is working as a cook in a little restaurant, working ten or eleven hours a day.

She is barely making ends meet. It is wrong that people who aren't working are getting more money than she is. I think she ought to get to keep more of what she earns. I don't think it's fair that because she is working, she gets no medical coverage, or has difficulty getting it, and somebody who doesn't work gets the best in the world.[3]

Senator Gramm is right to say that the government treats the working poor unfairly.[4] But his "compassion" for them has not been expressed by granting them greater access to medical care, but by taking it away from the poor mothers who have it. The "welfare reform" Gramm and the Republicans have favored substantially reduces help to the first group and takes away part of the very modest aid to the second group. That might succeed in forcibly transferring families from the first to the second group, but it would not reduce the number of children in dire circumstances and would deepen the deprivation of many. Senator Gramm does speak of allowing the minimum-wage cook to keep more of what she earns, by which he presumably means she should pay lower taxes. However, no tax rebate would be able to fully meet the health-care and child-care needs of her children.

Giving substantial additional aid with child care and health care to families in the second group would enable single parents with low skills to maintain a job whose wages, combined with the benefits, would provide a decent standard of living. It would give families in the first group an incentive to move into the second group. As we have seen with France, it is possible, through greater financial commitment and a wider base of political support, to design policies that protect children from poverty, that encourage work, and that keep families together. Without some movement in that direction, the United States is unlikely to make much progress in alleviating child poverty.

MAJOR AMERICAN PROGRAMS AIDING FAMILIES WITH CHILDREN

French programs to improve child well-being grew out of that country's unique history. In trying to use France's experience to think of ways we might better our own system, it is helpful to look at the details of our programs, the history that shaped them, and the rules that govern their operations. Some, such as the Earned

Income Tax Credit, which has no close counterpart in France, can be thought of as filling some of the same needs as French programs of income supplementation. Others, such as those for parents who stay home with their children—AFDC—have closer French counterparts but are less used in France because that country has programs that encourage parents to hold jobs. Perhaps the most important differences between the two countries are in the history and operation of their child-care and medical-care programs. An effective American program to redress child poverty will have to involve a decisive change in these two areas.

Aid to Families with Dependent Children

The main program for supplementing the income of poor families with children has been AFDC, popularly known as "welfare." It is designed to support single mothers who stay home with their children and do not hold substantial jobs. In all states but Alaska, U.S. welfare benefits, even supplemented by food stamps, are not generous enough to lift the families that qualify for them up to the official poverty line, or even to get them close to it.[5] AFDC has its origins in the Social Security Act of 1935, which also established the public pension system and unemployment insurance. Like the other programs under the act, it has been an "entitlement," which means that every family meeting the formal requirements has been provided with benefits, something not true for federal housing and child-care programs.

Each state has been allowed to set its own level of AFDC benefits; in 1994, the median monthly state grant to a mother with two children and no other income was $366.[6] The variation in benefit levels among states has been quite large. Mississippi had a maximum AFDC benefit for a mother and two children of $120 per month in 1994, while Connecticut gave $680 and Alaska gave $923. The federal government and the states have shared the cost of AFDC benefits. In better-off states, the federal share has been 50 percent, but for states with low per-capita income, the federal share has gone as high as 79 percent.[7] Differences in living costs, particularly costs for housing and winter heat, and differences in the tax-paying capacities of the states' citizens, account for some of the variation among states' benefit levels. But benefit levels also reflect the state governments' radically differing attitudes toward government help for poor people. (The most closely comparable French program, the API, provided $837).

An AFDC client who gets a job receives a reduced benefit. While some small amount of outside income is exempt, the general rule is that each dollar earned reduces the AFDC benefit by a dollar. As a result, the benefit of work at low wages is small. This discourages job-holding and has the effect of keeping the benefits tightly focused on those who earn nothing, or at least report that they earn nothing.[8]

In 1991, AFDC benefits cost the federal government $11.1 billion and the states $10.2 billion, while administration of the program cost $2.7 billion. There were 12.5 million recipients in that year, of whom 8.5 million were children. Of all unmarried mothers on AFDC, 46 percent had only one child, and another 30 percent had two. AFDC recipients were 5.05 percent of the total population; of all children, 13.2 percent were in the program.[9]

In Pennsylvania, where the level of benefits is modestly above the average, a mother with two children who reported no earnings received the maximum AFDC grant of $5,052 per year in 1994. Additional children would each raise annual benefits by about $1,080. Benefits are also available to families with both mother and father present, provided neither parent is employed and the father has a history of job-holding. However, only 9 percent of benefits under the program have gone to two-parent families.[10]

The welfare program was started in the United States in the 1930s, at a time when it was unusual for a mother of any but the lowest socioeconomic status to work. Being a domestic worker in someone else's home was the only job that was available to many women. Welfare was intended to save mothers who had lost their spouses and who, in the depths of the Great Depression, had little chance of finding a decent job to support themselves and their children. At the outset, local officials, especially in the southern states where most blacks lived, were able to keep black mothers' participation in the AFDC program low by outright discrimination, with little or no interference from the federal government.[11] Because discrimination against black men limited their earnings potential, many black mothers were already working as maids, and program administrators had no desire to help them leave their jobs.

The postwar period saw a decrease in federal tolerance of the discriminatory exclusion of eligible black families from the AFDC rolls. Since black men and black women continued to have the worst access to well-paying jobs, and had the highest rate of single parenthood, it was natural that the black share of AFDC recipients would rise. Another development in the postwar period was the large and continuous increase in the proportion of mothers in the labor force. The mother-at-home ceased to be the norm during the 1970s. Both the stay-at-home wife and the mother dependent on AFDC were increasingly seen as having chosen their jobless status over the respectable alternative of job holding. A great irony in the welfare debate is that while some have seen the housewife's choice as a legitimate and even admirable renunciation of her own interests for the children's sake, the single mother who stays home has been accused of shirking her responsibilities to herself and her children.

With these postwar changes, and with the increasing incidence of single parenthood among both blacks and whites, public antagonism against AFDC and its recipients has grown. This was especially true during the administrations of Republican presidents from Nixon on, all of whom tailored their messages to appeal to white conservative voters. President Reagan was particularly adept at encouraging the public to think of welfare recipients as loafers and cheats.

The political rhetoric from both Republicans and Democrats suggests that a majority of the population would now like to change our method of helping single parents, to reduce, if possible, the encouragement to form single-parent families and to reduce the proportion of single parents without jobs. Bill Clinton's proposals have included putting a time limit on the receipt of AFDC benefits and increasing the availability of job training and job placement for AFDC recipients. Job training and placement programs have been tried many times before with little or no success.

While some "theorists" have advocated terminating all help to single parents,[12] the Republicans in Congress have favored a less radical plan. They advocate turning the welfare program over to the states to run with whatever eligibility rules they please, with help from a federal block grant that would give each state a fixed amount of federal dollars for the program. The Republicans would reduce the program's resources, and they would end AFDC's entitlement feature, leaving in doubt states' ability to handle sudden increases in the number of eligible clients that might occur in recessions.

The Food Stamp Program

The food stamp program, which distributes stamps that can be exchanged for food, is funded almost entirely by the federal government. There is no comparable program in France. The U.S. program originated in the desire of liberals to supplement the income of all poor people, regardless of their marital status or whether they had children. Its passage was aided by claims that large numbers of people in the United States, including many children, were suffering from hunger and malnutrition. Legislators from the normally conservative farming states have supported the program on the theory that it increases the demand for their constituents' products. The food stamp program has been treated as an entitlement: anyone fulfilling the eligibility requirements is guaranteed the legal benefit. Until recently, the food stamp program has been free from political attack. However, some current Republican "reform" proposals would decentralize its operation and eliminate its entitlement status.

In 1993, 28.4 million people benefited from the food stamp program, and the average annual per-person benefit was $816. Just under half of all food stamp recipients were also AFDC beneficiaries.[13] Families in states with low AFDC benefits get modestly larger food stamp benefits under federally set formulas, which are not at state discretion.

A Pennsylvania single mother of two on the maximal AFDC grant received $2,496 worth of food stamps in 1994. If food stamps were the equivalent of money, that would bring her "income" to $7,548. However, evidence from consumer expenditure surveys suggests they are worth less to her than their face value. Single-mother families, on average, would have to have an annual income of about $20,000 before they would voluntarily spend that much for food eaten at home.[14] If she is typical, our Pennsylvania AFDC client would prefer to substitute other goods for a substantial share of the at-home food items she can buy with the stamps. Preventing her from doing so by restricting what the stamps can buy is not necessarily bad public policy. The public may wish to make sure that a poor family has better food than they would choose to buy. Benefits in the form of food may be politically easier to establish and maintain in the United States than the cash benefits that France prefers, so giving recipients benefits in kind may be the best that can be done for them.

The food stamp program and its recipients are highly visible to the public, because the stamps must be presented at the cash register of the store. At the checkout counter, the purchases of the food stamp recipients (including any alcoholic beverages, for which the stamps cannot be used) are wide open to view. Newspapers, radio talk shows, and television shows carry resentful comments by non-recipients who report having observed food stamp recipients buying liquor and other items that the nonrecipients cannot afford.

The Earned Income Tax Credit

The Earned Income Tax Credit (EITC) is designed to provide a cash supplement to working parents with low incomes.[15] It thus represents a move away from the policy of concentrating benefits on the single, at-home mother. The credit, by improving the standard of living for parents who earn very low wages, provides AFDC recipients with a very modest increase in the incentive to look for a job. President Clinton said during his campaign that people who have full-time jobs should be able to live above the poverty line. The EITC has up to now been the principal vehicle for moving toward that goal. In a country that has become increasingly conservative, and has shown increasing resistance to redistributing income from the well-off to the poor, the program has generally drawn little fire.[16] This is probably the result of the pro-work rhetoric of its proponents and the successful camouflage of a cash benefit as a tax break.

The EITC was originally enacted in 1975; at that time the benefit was calculated at 10 percent of parents' annual wage, up to a maximum of $400 a year.[17] The number of children did not affect the benefit level. By 1991, subsequent legislative acts had raised the benefit to 16.7 percent of wages for a family with one child and 17.3 percent for families with more than one, with a maximum benefit of $1,192 and $1,234, respectively. In 1993, a significant jump in benefits was mandated, to be phased in through 1996. By the end of 1996, the benefit for the one-child and multichild families was to be 34 percent and 40 percent of the wage, up to a maximum of $2,094 and $3,560, respectively. In 1995, however, the budget-cutting proposals included a reduction in EITC benefits.

As of 1991, 13 million families received EITC benefits totaling $9.4 billion. The average credit was $808, suggesting that a considerable proportion of beneficiaries worked part-time or were out of a job for part of the year.

Figure 6.1 charts the "structure" of the EITC benefits, with the benefit levels enacted for 1996. For the multichild family, the basic credit peaks at an annual wage income of $8,425, close to what is earned by a person working full-time, year-round, at the minimum wage of $4.25 an hour. Thus, the families getting less than the maximum benefit have wages from only a single part-time job. Families with incomes between $8,425 and $11,000 get the identical maximum benefit; for higher incomes the benefits are lowered, ceasing entirely for a family with an income of $27,000 or more. The law has provided that benefit levels increase automatically as the cost of living rises, so that their purchasing power would not be altered by inflation.[18]

Potential EITC recipients must apply for the credit on the federal income tax return form each year. If the credit due is smaller

FIGURE 6.1 BENEFIT LEVELS FOR A FAMILY WITH TWO OR MORE
CHILDREN UNDER THE EARNED INCOME TAX CREDIT, NEW
LAW VERSUS OLD LAW FOR TAX YEAR 1996

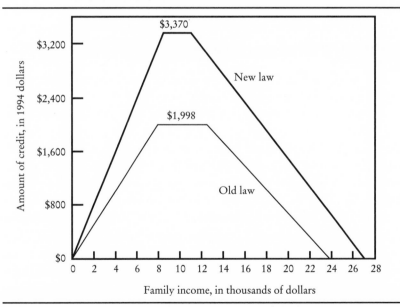

Source: Paul Leonard and Robert Greenstein, "The New Budget Reconciliation Law: Progressive Deficit Reduction and Critical Social Investments" (Washington: Center on Budget and Policy Priorities, n.d.).

than the tax owed, the credit is subtracted from the tax. If the credit is larger than the tax owed, the family gets the difference in cash; thus the EITC is said to be "refundable." Of the benefits paid based on 1991 earnings, 26 percent were received in the form of reduced income taxes and 74 percent were received in cash.[19]

Between 10 and 20 percent of those entitled to an EITC fail to get it, probably because they fail to file an income tax return.[20] For those who do apply, the entire benefit is most often received in one lump sum when the family files its annual tax return. As a result, many families are not able to integrate it into their regular monthly budget, and the benefit may be dissipated on items of secondary value to the family. Efforts are being made to divide at least part of the annually determined benefits into monthly payments, as well as to increase the percentage of eligible families who actually file for and receive the benefit.

Because of its name, and because one must make a claim to the EITC on the federal income tax return, the EITC appears in the guise of a tax break, one of the few angled toward the poor and near-poor. However, the refundability feature makes it the equivalent of a cash benefit. Perhaps the EITC has been presented as a tax break because the tax-allergic American public is more supportive of tax breaks than of benefit payments to low-income citizens. As a tax break, increases in the EITC have passed without public controversy.

The EITC, since it is the equivalent of a cash benefit, has some similarity to the family allowances that France and many other European countries provide. However, it cuts out at a relatively low level of income. Most European countries pay a family allowance benefit whose size depends only on the number of children, and not on the size of the family income, although most of them also have additional benefit programs that do vary with income.[21]

France and other countries find it administratively convenient simply to send a family allowance check monthly or quarterly, while the EITC, if it comes monthly, comes at the workplace as an addition to take-home pay. Europeans who are used to getting a monthly family allowance check understand that they get it whether they have a job or not. For this reason, the parents currently on welfare-like programs in Europe are not discouraged from work by the potential loss of this benefit. In the United

States, many parents on welfare may not know that the EITC will be added to their take-home pay if they take a low-wage job, but they do know that their welfare benefit will be lost. Thus, the EITC's potential incentive to job-holding is somewhat blunted.

Other Income Tax Breaks to Families with Children

The federal tax code contains two other provisions that provide help to families with children. For each child, it exempts $2,350 from income subject to income tax. Since the tax rate rises with income, better-off families get more, to a maximum credit of $940 per child. However, the exemption is reduced for top-earning families. This provision allowed forgiveness of taxes worth $21 billion in 1991; similar state exemptions are estimated to have added another $4.4 billion.[22] Second, the federal tax code provides a tax credit that offsets a minor portion of child-care expenditures. These tax concessions help only those families that have enough income to owe some federal or state income tax. They do not help the poorest families—those who have low-wage jobs or those suffering significant unemployment in the course of a calendar year.

Housing Assistance

Low-income families in the United States are generally not home-owners, so cannot take advantage of the main government housing assistance, the income tax deduction for home mortgage interest. Housing aid to them comes in the form of low-rent apartments in publicly owned apartment buildings, rent subsidies for government-designated units in privately owned buildings, and vouchers that families can use for part of their rent in the unit of their choice. Families or individuals are eligible for housing assistance if they have an income that is lower than 50 percent of the median income in their area.[23] Because of the variation among states in median income, the income cutoff for these programs for a four-person family ranges from $12,000 in rural Mississippi to $36,700 in metropolitan Connecticut.[24] The median income of a family in public housing in 1989 was $6,500, and for a family receiving a housing voucher, $7,600.[25] Although the programs have different benefits, a typical program would require the family to pay out of pocket a rent equivalent to 20–30 percent of its income, with the subsidy paying for the rest.

Housing aid is not an "entitlement," as AFDC, food stamps, and Medicaid are. That means that the appropriations for housing aid are not automatically fixed at a level that would give benefits to all eligible households. In fact, benefits in 1989 went to only 4.1 million households out of the 13.8 million households that were eligible. The result is that some households receive substantial benefits, while others in similar circumstances receive nothing at all. While 1.8 million households with children received benefits, 4.2 million eligible households with children were not helped.

The housing programs are not particularly targeted toward families with children; many recipients are elderly individuals or couples. Of all households receiving housing assistance, 45 percent have children, which is about the same as the proportion of households with children among all eligible households.[26] We can estimate that, in 1991, families with children received $8.5 billion worth of help with housing. Thus, these programs make a substantial contribution to the benefits currently flowing toward children in the United States. However, the French housing assistance to families with children was more extensive still, amounting to the equivalent of $22.6 billion for a country the size of the United States. (See table 4.1.)

As is well known, living in assisted housing in the United States is not an unalloyed benefit. Many of the units are in housing projects plagued by drug traffic, and crime rates are high. Upkeep is poor in some projects; in 1989, 12 percent of public housing residents reported that they had no working toilet at some time within the previous three months, 18 percent reported water leakage, and 12 percent reported signs of rats.[27]

Medicaid

The federal government has required all states to run a Medicaid program that pays for medical services to AFDC recipients. Also eligible for Medicaid as of 1994 are all other children born since 1983 (but not their parents) whose family income is below the official poverty line, and children under six in families with incomes less than 133 percent of the poverty line. Pregnant women with income under 133 percent of the poverty line must also be covered, but only for pregnancy-related care. States are permitted to cover pregnant women and infants under one year with higher incomes. As of 1993, thirty-four states did so; of those, twenty-five states set their income limits at 185 percent of the poverty line, the maximum federal regulations allow.[28] Medicaid also pays the bills for elderly nursing home residents who have spent down their remaining assets.

The Medicaid program works by reimbursing providers of medical services, who agree to accept the state-set fee levels and who are allowed to collect only nominal copayments from patients covered by the program. Federal law requires states to set provider fees at a level that ensures such patients have the same access to services as the general public. However, this provision of the law is not always carried out in practice. The federal government and the states share Medicaid costs, with a federal share of 50 percent for better-off states and up to 83 percent for the poorer states. The program pays for physician services, hospital stays, laboratory tests, and family planning services and supplies. State programs can also pay for prescription drugs, eyeglasses, dental services, and medical transportation, and almost all states do so. In 1992, the average Medicaid expenditure was $998 for an AFDC child and $1,753 for an AFDC adult.[29]

Like cash benefits, government-provided health insurance in the United States is concentrated on families of single parents without jobs. Employed Americans are expected to get health insurance through their employer; however, a substantial fraction of employed people do not receive it, including many poorly educated single mothers. The self-employed must also purchase their own health insurance. Unlike France's national health insurance program, which covers all legal residents and medical costs, the Medicaid program leaves many gaps in coverage, even for the very poorest children, as table 6.2 shows. Between the gaps in Medicaid and some employers' failure to provide health insurance, 14 percent of American children, or about ten million, mostly the offspring of "working poor" adults, are not covered.[30]

The Medicaid program has been a great source of fiscal grief to the states and the federal government, because of sharply rising costs. Those delivering health services, including physicians, hospitals, and even taxicab companies paid to take poor, disabled people to medical visits, have billed the program for services that have been unnecessary or undelivered. The Republican drive to reduce expenditures on the poor was meant to result in a curtailment of Medicaid expenditures, which would increase the numbers of peo-

TABLE 6.2 HEALTH INSURANCE COVERAGE FOR CHILDREN UNDER
MEDICAID, BY AGE AND POVERTY STATUS, 1992 (PERCENTAGE
WITH COVERAGE)

Age (Years)	Family Income in Relation to Official Poverty Line		
	Below the Poverty Line	100–133 Percent of Poverty Line	133–185 Percent of Poverty Line
0–5	73.7%	42.9%	27.4%
6–18	58.8	26.6	13.4

Source: U.S. House of Representatives, Committee on Ways and Means, *1994 Greenbook* (Washington: Government Printing Office, 1994), 788.

ple without insurance and reduce services for those who remain covered. However, efforts to transfer Medicaid recipients from fee-for-service insurance plans to health maintenance organizations (HMOs) that emphasize prevention and can better coordinate a family's health services may have positive results for both costs and patients' well-being if carried out responsibly.

Child Support Enforcement

When parents split up and the children remain with their mother, the per capita income in the mother's household is likely to be considerably lower than the per capita income in the father's household. The father's income would be four times as large as the per capita income of the mother's household in the typical case where two children live with their mother, the father lives alone, and the mother earns 70 percent of what the father earns. For this reason, child support payments have considerable potential to improve children's living standards.

All states in the United States have laws requiring parents to support their children. Where a parent lives apart from a child, and the biological relationship has been legally established, the resident parent may seek a court order to require the nonresident parent to make regular payments to help with the child's living costs.

The flow of child support payments has historically been far below its potential level. In many cases, paternity is never established, and a court order for support payments is never sought. In the past, judges have had total freedom to set award levels, and many have set levels that do not reflect a fair share of the child's cost to the resident parent. After the award level is set, delinquency in making payments is common, because nonpayment has typically brought no penalty. Census Bureau studies have consistently found that about half of resident parents have no awards, and that, of those who do, about half get all the payments to which they are entitled.[31] It is particularly difficult to enforce awards when the children reside in one state and the nonresident parent lives in another, which accounts for about one-third of all cases.

The Family Support Act of 1988 was one of a series of legislative attempts to improve the collection of child support payments. It encourages states to increase the number of paternity determinations, mandates state guidelines for award amounts, and requires that employers deduct child support payments from the pay of nonresident parents, and send them to a public authority, which in turn disburses them to the resident parent.

Irwin Garfinkel has suggested a further evolution of the system that in some ways echoes the French system for assuring child support.[32] He advocates that a universal formula be used for fixing child support obligation: 17 percent of the nonresident parent's gross income for one child, 25 percent for two, 29 percent for three, 31 percent for four, and up to 34 percent for five or more. The obligation therefore depends on the nonresident parent's income, in the manner of a tax. Payments would be collected by payroll deductions and disbursed by a government agency, similar to the French system. A key element in Garfinkel's proposed program is "child support assurance": the government must make a minimum payment to the resident parent, even if that amount is not collected from the nonresident parent, either because the latter's income is too low or for any other reason.

Garfinkel's proposed system might replace welfare at lower cost to the taxpayers, since a considerable share of the support for single-parent families would be shifted from the taxpayers to the nonresident parents. Even more important, unlike welfare dollars, child support dollars would not be lost when the resident parent gets a job. So child support payments would have less of a deterrent effect on job-holding. Moreover, they could augment the income of the "second group" of families—single parents holding jobs that pay less than $20,000—thus helping those now of the "working poor" to live at a more comfortable standard.

*Care and Development Programs for Children Under
Age Six*

Americans spent $23.9 billion of public money in 1991 for care and
development programs that serve children below the first-grade
level.[33] This includes expenditures for infant and toddler care,
child-care centers and preschools for children out of diapers, Head
Start, and public kindergarten. Kindergarten and Head Start are not
usually included in tallies of child care, but they can serve a child-
minding function for working parents if they run all day, or if they
are on a half-day schedule and arrangements can be made to deliver
children to and from other forms of care as done in France.[34] Moreover, high-quality child-care programs for children out of diapers
include the kinds of developmental activities that go on in kindergartens and Head Start programs.

Kindergarten   By far the largest government spending on child
care and development in the United States goes for public
kindergarten. Virtually all public elementary schools in the United
States provide kindergarten classes. Most kindergartens in the
United States operate on a half-day schedule and are available in
most localities only to five-year olds, who attend in large numbers.
(See table 6.3.) Kindergarten teachers are required to have the same
training as teachers in the elementary grades. Kindergartens aim at
getting the children ready for school, giving them character and
behavior training, and improving their social skills. The kindergarten also tries to give special help to children from deprived
backgrounds.[35] In a typical kindergarten classroom, "areas" are set
up for such activities as math, science, sociodramatic play, reading,
writing, and arts.[36]

    Half-day kindergarten classes, unlike school grades one through
twelve, provide little or no help with child care to parents who
hold a job. However, the availability of full-day kindergarten has
increased slowly but steadily; of five-year-olds attending private
and public kindergartens, 42 percent went to a full-day program in
1992, up from the 12 percent going full-day in 1965.[37]

Head Start   Head Start, a service-intensive nursery school program for the country's poorest children, is a remnant of President
Lyndon Johnson's Great Society anti-poverty program, and probably the only part of that program that is today in good repute

TABLE 6.3 ENROLLMENT OF CHILDREN AGES THREE TO FIVE YEARS IN
PREPRIMARY PROGRAMS IN THE UNITED STATES, 1992

	Percent Enrolled by Age of Child		
Preschool Program	Three Years	Four Years	Five Years
Nursery school			
Public	9%	16%	4%
Private	18	26	3
Kindergarten			
Public	1	7	70
Private	1	3	10
Enrollees who attend full-day	34	32	42

Source: National Center for Education Statistics, *Digest of Educational Statistics, 1993* (Washington, 1993), 62.

across the political spectrum. Many poor children, it was realized, enter school without the knowledge, skills, habits, and health necessary to succeed there. The program tries to improve their social and cognitive skills and to attend to any nutritional, health, or fitness deficits that can be detected. Head Start teachers try to work with the parents to improve their nurturing skills. Children who attend Head Start programs perform better on tests of cognitive skills than those who do not attend, although some studies have found that differences disappear within a few years.[38]

About two-thirds of the children Head Start enrolls are four-year olds, and most of the rest are three. After its founding in 1965, Head Start enrollments were flat or falling during the 1970s, but grew modestly in the conservative 1980s. In 1993 the program enrolled 713,903 children and spent $2.8 billion, or $3,758 per child.[39]

Head Start providers are local public agencies or private nonprofit groups or school systems that get funding from and are supervised by the federal Head Start program. Federal regulations require two paid staff persons (a teacher and a teacher aide or two teachers) for each class, the size of which is restricted to twenty five-year-olds, or seventeen younger children. The teachers are required to have college degrees in early childhood education or to have obtained a Child Development Associate credential, requiring 120 hours of formal training and 480 hours of experience.[40] However, 19 percent of them were lacking such qualifications in 1993.[41]

Head Start providers are required to fill 90 percent of their slots with children from families at or below the poverty line, so they can offer services to only the lowest-paid parents. Even if broader eligibility were established, however, Head Start in its present form could not serve the child-care needs of parents who hold full-time jobs because, like the majority of kindergartens, it operates on a part-year and part-day schedule, and parents are required to attend some sessions in person. The funds appropriated have been insufficient to give all eligible children even a single year's service, so multiple-year enrollments are seldom available. Proposals to make Head Start a full-year, all-day program, and to expand eligibility to children under 150 percent of the poverty line, have not been acted on.[42] In 1995, Republican proposals for welfare reform included provisions that would relegate Head Start funding to block grants to the states, which could continue the program or use the funds in some other way.

Other Child-Care Programs   Since the administration of President Nixon, a long line of programs have been designed to get women off the welfare rolls by getting them into jobs. The current incarnation is called Job Opportunities and Basic Skills (JOBS), which was created under the Family Support Act of 1988. These programs have emphasized training for work readiness, but they have also offered transitional help (usually for a year) with health insurance and child care for women leaving welfare for work. JOBS programs also offer child care to job-holding mothers in danger of going on welfare because they cannot afford to pay for child care. In addition, a large number of small specialized programs offer child care as part of their array of services. In 1994, the General Accounting Office (GAO) issued a report identifying no fewer than ninety "early childhood" programs (all small) supervised by thirty-one federal agencies, and criticized the proliferation of separate programs and their overlapping functions.[43]

Public Funding for Child Care

In the face of low public provision of child care to help parents with full-time jobs, a highly variegated private child-care industry has grown up in the United States as women's participation in paid work has risen. Private child-care providers include both nonprofit groups and profit-making corporations, some of which operate chains of centers. A considerable number of child-care centers are connected to religious institutions. The prevailing practice in the industry is to pay low wages, which attracts only workers with few alternatives, encourages high turnover, and creates problems with quality.[44] A considerable part of the industry consists of so-called family day-care providers—individual women, mostly mothers, who take children into their homes. In 1991, 42 percent of the children not receiving care from parents or relatives were in family day care. Only an estimated 10–20 percent of family day-care operators are licensed and regulated.[45] Unlike France which offers incentives to family day-care providers to come under regulation, no such efforts are being made in the United States. Many unlicensed providers illegally evade payroll and income taxes. That allows them to offer low prices and may be one of the reasons that the centers, which must compete with the family day-care providers, keep costs down by paying low wages.

The lack of public help with child care creates a difficult financial burden for American parents of preschool children, whether the family pays for care or the mother or another relative stays at home and forgoes earnings. For those single mothers who do not have access to a well-paying job and who lack a relative willing and able to donate care, financing good-quality child care is literally impossible. These mothers are faced with a set of bad choices: a life on AFDC or putting their children into low-quality care that nevertheless makes a huge hole in their pocket. Even solidly middle-class families must choose between settling for subpar care and paying a price they consider out of their range.

While there have been many calls over the years for government help with child care, conservatives—who favor low taxes and oppose enlarging the public sector—have offered spirited resistance. Similarly, those who want women to return to traditional roles generally oppose government-assisted child care. Whenever public child-care proposals appear to enjoy significant political support, opponents propose putting the money instead into cash benefits or tax credits labeled "for child care," but that can be spent on anything the family wishes. They argue that parents who care for their own children at home would be "discriminated against" if they were denied the government help that job-holding mothers would get from government subsidies to child care.

Some opposition to out-of-home child care is based on the belief that such care is inferior to in-home care. Researchers who have looked at the effect of out-of-home care on children do not find evidence that such care is necessarily harmful:

> Child care settings were traditionally viewed as environments that, by comparison with children's own homes, were deficient as contexts for development. [Our review of the evidence] present[s] a different picture. Family day care and center care can be environments that effectively support children's health and development. They can also provide some unique opportunities for enhancing development (e.g., for peer interactions, cognitive interventions, cultural affirmation). Yet existing evidence from research and professional practice forces us to face an important caveat: child care supports healthy physical and psychological development only when it is of high quality.[46]

The concern about quality is a serious one. A recent study of child-care centers, led by Suzanne Helburn, found that "[c]hild care at most centers in the United States is poor to mediocre, with almost half of the infants and toddlers [children under three] in rooms having less than minimal quality."[47] The researchers found that quality care costs more, but not a lot more. They recommended higher licensing standards and an end to exemptions from state regulations for centers under religious auspices. They also urged increased financial support by the government and higher pay and better training for child-care personnel. They believe that a good standard of care is achievable in the United States, and they endorse the proposition that all children and their families should have access to such care.[48]

Proponents of government help with child care have been weakened by internal dissension, particularly on religious issues. The Supreme Court has up to now interpreted the American constitutional principle of the separation of church and state as a prohibition against public funding for religious schools in grades one through twelve. Whether child-care facilities under religious auspices could or should receive public funds is still an open question; presumably the Court might decide that they are more closely analogous to church hospitals, which do receive public funds, than to church schools, which do not. However, religious groups are already supplying (and selling to parents) a considerable amount of child care and would like to receive public subsidies. They actively oppose any program providing government financial support for child care that would exclude their programs from participating.

Profit-making child-care centers do not want to see their market invaded by no-fee, government-run child-care centers, want to be eligible for subsidies, and want to be able to receive children whose parents pay with government vouchers. Managers of nonprofit providers also have an interest in protecting their institutions against government displacement or competition. On the other hand, public school proponents, including their unions and administrators, would like to see the public school system branch out into care for preschool children and become the central provider. They have opposed a voucher system that would pay for private child care, because that would strengthen the current campaign to institute voucher systems for kindergarten through grade twelve.

A bill with provisions for federal support for child-care activities passed the U.S. Congress in 1971, but was vetoed by President Nixon.[49] President Ford vetoed another child-care bill in 1974. Title XX of the Social Security Act, passed in 1975, provided the states with grants for social services for the low-income population that included a small set-aside for child care. In 1981 and thereafter, Title XX moneys were treated as block grants, and the states were free to allocate them as they wished. States could use these funds for child care, but they were not required to do so. About 70 percent of them devote part of the funds to child care. Perhaps 400,000 children are provided with care under Title XX, which sets no federal quality standards. That constitutes less than 3 percent of the population of poor children.[50]

In 1990, a coalition of advocates for public help with child care led by the Children's Defense Fund—which included labor unions, parent advocacy groups, and groups concerned with child welfare and early childhood education—were able to engineer the provision of federal funds to the states specifically designated for child care. The Child Care and Development Block Grant (CCDBG) was included in the 1990 Budget Act, which was signed by President Bush. It also required states to establish quality standards. The appropriations allowed for the CCDBG were quite modest—$732 million for 1991 and slightly larger amounts for the two subsequent years.[51] However the act did strengthen the principle of a federal role in out-of-home child care and increased federal funding for its support.

The CCDBG funds go to the states, who administer them under federal guidelines. Children are eligible to attend a CCDBG-funded program if they are under thirteen, and if their family income is no greater than 75 percent of a state's median income. Each state designates a lead agency, through which child-care providers get grant funds. These funds enable the providers to offer places to eligible children. After-school facilities for "latchkey children" can be also funded under the act, and part of the funds were earmarked for quality improvements. Profit-making centers were allowed to receive children benefiting under the act.

The CCDBG allows child-care centers under religious auspices to take part in the program, which means that taxpayers are supporting child care that includes sectarian activities. It also allows providers to exclude employees on religious grounds and to consider the parents' religion when deciding which children to admit. These provisions, which reduced opposition from Catholics, Orthodox Jews, and some Christian fundamentalists, will be tested in lawsuits alleging that they violate the Constitution's requirement of separation between church and state.

In the recent spate of welfare reform efforts, most states, backed by some federal funds, are offering programs that provide full-time care for some of the children of mothers who leave welfare. These programs are limited in most cases to a single year, with the stated purpose of "weaning people off welfare." Other programs provide child care to those designated "in danger" of going on welfare. Only single mothers with very low wages can use these programs, and they cannot count on them for the entire period in which they have pre-elementary school children.

The disjointed and miserly qualities of U.S. child-care efforts compare poorly with France's generously supported child-care programs, in which nearly all families with children benefit. The American public programs of "child care and development" are mostly half-day programs whose focus is development. They offer little or no help with the kind of care that is useful to parents who have jobs, as the French system does. Moreover, the appropriations voted for child-care programs do not begin to address the needs of families with children in the bottom third of the income distribution. The recent legislative "victories" of child-care proponents have done little to help lower-income parents and virtually nothing to help middle-class parents with their child-care problems.

Four Species of Reform

One could imagine that the public opprobrium attached to single mothers who do not hold a job might translate into honor and generosity toward those who do work. But it does not. As we have seen, parents who try to help themselves by holding a job are entitled to government benefits that are far less generous than the benefits for non–job holders. The present system of U.S. programs for families with children both creates disincentives for job holding and leaves millions of children in poverty.

Conservatives would cut off benefits to many single mothers, drastically reduce the benefits to others, and restrict the time period such benefits could be received. This would certainly increase the incentive for these mothers to work and might reduce the number of births to women without sources of male support. However, many mothers would be unable to support their children adequately on the pay they would get; some might not be able to secure steady work and would be highly vulnerable during recessions. So raising the incentive to work would not solve the problem of their poverty.

A second type of reform would involve eliminating the big advantage that welfare has over low-wage work by better subsidizing low-wage work. This would mean increasing still further the Earned Income Tax Credit, which would reduce poverty and improve the incentive to get a job.

A third line of attack would be to institute a French-style family allowance for families with children (disguised as a refundable tax credit), which would give extra cash to all families with children, regardless of their income. While this program would broaden the base of support for help to families with children, most of the funds would add to the incomes of relatively well-off people. This program would modestly improve the incentive to work, because, as is true in France, single parents would retain most of their cash benefits if they took a job. This approach has been the preferred policy direction of groups that advocate for poor children.

A fourth species of reform would provide the "big ticket" services of child care and health care to families with children. Such a program would provide larger benefits to low-income families than they would receive through universal family allowances. It would reduce poverty among children and improve work incentives, and it would guarantee that children get high-quality care. Since it would deliver services to children rather than cash to adult parents, it might be more popular than other suggested reforms. A program of this type would guarantee that all families with children have health insurance, and it would fully subsidize child care for low-income families and partially subsidize it for middle-income families. The details of such a program are presented in the next chapter.

✤ CHAPTER 7 ✤

Reducing Child Poverty by Helping Working Parents

HOW ARE WE to design and pay for a system of programs in the United States that would enable more families to live above the poverty line? As the previous chapters have shown, French programs accomplish this by giving a great deal of help to parents who hold low-paying jobs. In order to do that, the French spend heavily in three areas: providing child care, providing health care, and providing income supplements, including help with rent. A major theme of this chapter is that government help with child care and health insurance, covered by vouchers rather than by cash grants, are the necessary ingredients for protecting American children from deprivation.

Any system of programs will reflect the values of those devising the system. Many Americans put heavy weight on discouraging births outside of marriage and getting single parents to take jobs. The aim of reducing child poverty in the short and medium run goes largely unmentioned in the debate on reforming American welfare. On the other hand, many of those on the right appear willing to adopt policies that would increase child deprivation in the short run, on the ground that treating single parents harshly will teach them and others not to produce more children destined to be poor.

The French clearly put the greatest weight on keeping all children out of deprivation and do not put a great deal of emphasis on reducing improvident births. In fact, most of the components of their child welfare system were constructed with French-born married couples in mind, in the apparently vain hope that they would be induced to have more children. The unmarried are eligible for all of these pronatally motivated benefits, which—if they have an effect on births to unwed couples—might be expected to increase rather than reduce such births. On the other hand, increasing the labor force participation of single mothers, as these benefits do, may have a negative effect on the number of children they have, since women in jobs generally desire fewer children than those who do not.[1] As we have seen, birthrates outside marriage are very similar in France and the United States, suggesting that the more generous benefits to single parents in France have not resulted in a flood of children to unmarried couples. Nonetheless, an American system more like the French one might not discourage births as effectively as would reduced benefits, promoted by U.S. politicians on the right. A system along French lines would provide a single mother who has low labor-market skills with an option she does not have under the present system—she and her children could live above the poverty line, provided she works for pay.

Even though the French system has achieved both low child-poverty rates and relatively high job-holding among single parents, would it work in the United States, with its very different history and culture? The fact is, the basic needs of families in the two countries are not at all different. Whether they live in France or the United States, preschool children must be cared for—by parents, by other family members, or by paid nonrelatives. Good child care is expensive to buy or provide in both countries. American children, like French children, have health-care needs, which are met or not met depending on their access to care. Whatever the incentives parents have to take jobs, there will be parents in both countries with low wages or no wages. Even if child care and medical care are provided, such children live in families that need financial help to purchase sufficient food, clothing, and shelter.

What is different in the two countries is not children's needs, but the sense of public responsibility for the welfare of the nation's children, the feelings of generosity toward those who are poor, the willingness to pay taxes, racial antipathies, the proportion of public funds devoted to armaments, the degree of faith in the government's ability to deliver effective and high-quality programs, and beliefs about the importance and means of limiting "dysfunctional" behavior, such as births to unmarried teenage mothers. These attitudinal differences do not preclude the design of an effective American program to fight child poverty, but they do create roadblocks to the acceptance of such a program.

While the unsatisfactory state of current American programs for health care and income supplementation is well known, the child-care issue has only recently been recognized as an important component in solving the problem of child poverty. Critical to the argument that follows is the idea that health care and good-quality child care are "big-ticket items," and that most of the jobs open to women on welfare will not provide them as fringe benefits or, alternatively, do not pay high enough wages to enable their purchase.

COSTING OUT A FAMILY BUDGET

The design of a set of programs that would enable all children to live in decency must begin with an accounting of the family's needs. The assessment of needs is frequently equated to setting a poverty line. One might say that a family is "in poverty" when it has fewer resources than society deems necessary to avoid severe deprivation. We can then go on to inquire how those necessary resources might be supplied to families with children so as to discourage behavior that is unwise or costly to others.

The official methodology of computing a poverty-line income for the United States and of counting the families who fall below it —established in 1964—is widely understood to be flawed.[2] No attention is given to the differences between the needs of single-parent families and two-parent families, or among different single-parent families. The methodology used does not consider, for example, whether a single parent stays home with the children full-time, or holds a job entailing extra expenditures for child care, transportation, and direct taxes. The official method ignores tax obligations, and thus ignores the effect of income tax and social security tax on the size of the wage needed to provide a decent standard.[3] When the government classifies families as poor or non-poor under its official method, the family's receipt of any in-kind benefits is ignored.

These deficiencies mean that an alternative approach must be used to account in a realistic way for minimal family needs. The "Basic Needs Budget" (BNB) approach serves that purpose, by specifying an adequacy standard for each of the major groups of goods and services that families consume, and adding on an appropriate amount for direct taxes.[4] These standards call for health insurance, licensed child care for children of an age to require it, and undilapidated housing. Recently, a committee set up by the National Academy of Sciences recommended that the government adopt an approach similar to the BNB methodology in deciding who should be designated as poor.[5]

Table 7.1 presents Basic Needs Budgets for two single-mother families, each with two preschool children, living in an area with housing costs about average for the United States. The first column presents a budget for a family in which the mother stays home and cares for her own children full-time; the second column presents a budget for a family in which the single parent holds a full-time job. The bundle of basic goods and services, exclusive of health insurance, required by a single mother who holds down a job costs just about twice as much as the bundle required by the single mother who stays home. A minor amount of the increase in costs is for

TABLE 7.1 MONTHLY REQUIREMENTS FOR GOODS AND SERVICES, BASIC
NEEDS BUDGET FOR U.S. SINGLE-MOTHER FAMILIES, WITH
TWO PRESCHOOL CHILDREN, 1993

Goods and services	Parent full-time at home	Parent at full-time job
Food	$292	$292
Housing	357	357
Clothing	84	84
Transportation	39	85
Personal care and miscellaneous	58	58
Health care		
Health insurance provided by	Medicaid	Employer or government
Out-of-pocket health expenses	74	74
Paid child care	—	800
Monthly total, exclusive of health insurance	$904	$1,750
Annual total, exclusive of health insurance and child care	$10,848	$11,400

Source: For a detailed description of how the budget items were determined, see Trudi J. Renwick and Barbara R. Bergmann, "A Budget-Based Definition of Poverty, with an Application to Single-Parent Families," *Journal of Human Resources* 28 (Winter 1993): 1–24.

transportation to work; the major increase comes from the need for paid child care.

ACHIEVING A DECENT LIVING STANDARD

Table 7.2 lays out three alternative ways of providing the goods and services that the Basic Needs Budget allows for a single mother and two preschool children. It includes an accounting for the normal taxes that a wage earner would have to pay, and shows how additional government benefit programs might be grafted onto our present programs to allow the family to achieve the BNB standard.

TABLE 7.2 THREE METHODS OF PROVIDING A FAMILY CONSISTING OF A
SINGLE PARENT AND TWO PRESCHOOL CHILDREN WITH
ENOUGH RESOURCES TO BUY THE BASIC NEEDS BUDGET IN
1993

Needs	Total Independence	Parent at Home on Generous Stipend ("Full Welfare")	Help for Working Parents (HWP)
Cash income	Job paying $24,255	Welfare benefit, food stamps, etc. totaling $10,847	(1) Minimum-wage job, $8,840
			(2) Earned Income Tax Credit, $1,511
			(3) Food stamps, $1,900
Health insurance	Employer	Medicaid	HWP program
Child care	Purchased by family, 9,600	Provided by parent at home	Provided by HWP program
Taxes	3,255	—	851
Social security tax	1,856		676
Federal income tax	1,817		0
Dependent care credit	−1,056		0
State income tax	638		175
Cash available for other goods and services	11,400	10,847	11,400

Source: Calculations of benefits and taxes by the author.

These options would fulfill the mechanical requirement that resources sufficient for the BNB standard be provided. All of them are not achievable for everyone and not necessarily good from the public policy point of view. In fact, the first of the three—total independence—is unachievable for the majority of families headed by a single mother, because of labor market conditions. The second—a single parent at home on a generous stipend—would have undesirable consequences and is politically unachievable. The third—help for working parents—is broadly achievable, if certain conditions are met.

Total Independence

The first column in table 7.2 indicates how well a single job-holding mother would have to do in the labor market to maintain her two preschool children in decency. The figures present a "total independence" solution to the problem of child poverty. It displays the annual wage income a mother would require to achieve the BNB standard after paying federal, state, and social security taxes. Taxes add $3,255 to the $21,000 needed annually to buy goods and services. The budget on which this case is based (the second column of figures in table 7.1) assumes the mother holds a job in which the employer provides health insurance.

Jobs with a pre-tax wage of $24,255 or above are not available to all single mothers, given the state of the labor market. Of all women working full-time year-round in 1993, more than half earned less than $24,255; the median wage among these women workers was $20,540.[6] The scheduled improvement in the Earned Income Tax Credit would increase the proportion of single mothers able to finance the Basic Needs Budget, but a high proportion would continue to be unable to do so. Furthermore, the jobs available to mothers currently on AFDC would very likely pay even less than jobs held by all currently employed women because the mothers on AFDC are, on average, less educated, have less work experience, and are more likely to be black or Hispanic than women currently working in full time, year-round jobs, and are subject more often to discrimination as a result.

"Total independence" at a decent standard of living is simply not available under present labor market conditions to most women on welfare. Even if in response to the harsh incentives advocated by conservatives these women made the maximum possible effort, most of the child poverty would remain. Some analysts argue that we should not take the condition of the labor market as a given. They argue that the core of an attack on poverty problems should consist in government programs that produce dramatically improved take-home pay for the unskilled.[7] However, the increasing competition from low-wage countries, and the technological change which is increasing wage inequality make that route more doubtful of success and more expensive than one targeted on families with children.

Full Welfare

The second column in table 7.2 displays a solution that we can call the "full welfare solution," in which the parent stays home and receives a generous stipend. A mother with two children in a state with median benefits got $7,548 in AFDC and food stamp benefits in 1993.[8] She could buy the BNB bundle of goods and services costed out in the first column of table 7.1 with an additional $3,259 in cash benefits. We may note parenthetically that welfare—provided on condition that a child under 18 lives in the home and that no adult in the family holds a job of any substance—does provide resources for child care.

This solution to the child poverty problem has its adherents. They argue that a woman who devotes full time to being a mother is doing hard, honorable, and important work, and that any mother who does not have private support should be entitled to government support to allow her to be a full-time homemaker, if that is what she wishes.[9] However, the prevailing sentiment appears to be that the government should not offer a comfortable life for extended periods, exempt from job-holding, to mothers who lack private support, unless they are widows. In fact, the public apparently no longer wishes to continue supporting the subpar standard of living that welfare mothers now maintain.

Some of the demands from the right that single mothers take jobs possibly springs from punitive motives, especially among those who oppose the movement of married women into the labor force.[10] However, some of these demands come from those who believe that unmarried mothers should be as motivated to hold jobs as are the majority of married mothers. However, married mothers who enter the labor force are rewarded by their pay, less taxes and working expenses. Unmarried mothers on AFDC who enter the labor force are rewarded by their pay, less taxes, working expenses, and the welfare benefits they forgo.

The "full welfare solution" cannot be dismissed solely on the basis of its presumed unpopularity. Any solution that would save large numbers of children from poverty would be expensive and unlikely to find wide acceptance, at least without a long campaign in its favor. A more substantive argument against the "full welfare solution" is that its adoption would severely harm women by encouraging a return to the social system in force before the 1970s, when women's roles were perceived exclusively as childbearing and childrearing. A more generous stipend for single mothers at home would remove their incentive to join the labor market. It would discourage education. It would preclude them from independence, self-support, the community's respect, access to promotions into better jobs, the chance of financially successful and interesting careers, and interaction with adult peers. It would encourage them to go on having and caring for babies as a way of earning a good living. It would invite non–job-holding men to join their households as nonpaying guests, usurping resources intended for mothers and children. It would undercut still further the influence of parents on teenage children by offering teens a comfortable lifestyle independent of their parents and independent of the labor market. It would raise a demand that married women be supported with public funds to be housewives. It would reinforce the idea that women and men belong in separate spheres. In short, such a policy would deal a severe blow to the gains that women have made toward equality with men in opportunities and independence.

Help for Working Parents

A third approach to drastically reducing child poverty (shown in the third column of table 7.2) is to look at the situation of the mother in a full-time, year-round job at the current minimum wage and ask how government programs might provide her with enough supplementary resources to achieve the level of decency specified in the Basic Needs Budget.

The third column of table 7.2 shows one possible benefit package that would do the job. It includes an Earned Income Tax Credit of $1,511 and food stamps worth $1,900, both of which are currently mandated.[11] In addition, the family would receive health care, either from the employer or through a government program.

The package also includes a child-care benefit, in the form of access to government child-care facilities or vouchers accepted by non-government providers. (Accordingly, the cash budget for goods and services for this family does not include child-care costs.) Unless the family lives in a high-rent area, little or nothing in the way of additional cash benefits would be needed to bring this family up to the BNB requirements. We can call this the Help for Working Parents (HWP) solution.

The HWP solution would cost the public purse $15,909 for this three-person family.[12] That is $1,313 more than the "full welfare solution." Perhaps more to the point, the Help for Working Parents solution would cost $5,066 more than the government would have laid out in AFDC payments, food stamps, and Medicaid for a family of this size on welfare in 1993.[13] This $5,066 additional public expenditure would buy a higher standard of living for the family, a high-quality developmental day-care program for the children, and would enable the parent to take a job and assume the status of a worker. As previously noted, we might also expect that, on average, a woman holding a job would produce fewer children than a woman at home on AFDC.

The costs of an HWP program would be substantial even if the major new benefits—free or highly subsidized child care and health insurance—were restricted to those moving from welfare into jobs. However, as we have seen, a solution to the child poverty problem requires a substantial increase in help to those families with an annual wage income between $10,000 and $20,000. Much of the cost increase attached to HWP would be attributable to the rise in that group's benefits. Those working at low wages currently get no government benefits beyond a low allotment of food stamps and the Earned Income Tax Credit. The net additional cost to taxpayers of providing a two-child, non-AFDC, single-parent family with child care (at zero fee) and health insurance (assuming that the parent's job does not provide health insurance) would be $13,349.[14]

Help for Working Parents: Coverage and Features   As we have seen, if health care and child care are provided, then a year-round, full-time job at the minimum wage would allow a mother and two children to live in decency, if supplemented by the current Earned Income Tax Credit and food stamp programs and an expanded housing assistance program for families in high-rent areas. The program advocated here is built on that finding.

The child-care and health care benefits of the HWP program would go to married and unmarried parents, so that marriage would not be discouraged. It could not with any justice or coherence be restricted to those coming off welfare. If it were, parents with preschool children who had made the effort to support themselves with wages would, as now, see those who had not made that effort getting benefits worth thousands a year. We would have the unseemly sight of parents going on welfare for the purpose of getting valuable benefits when they left again. The unpopularity of the present system is in part due to this kind of lack of parity in treatment, and it should not be perpetuated if the new system is to gain support. Extending benefits beyond the very lowest income groups into the middle class increases the cost, but it also avoids the harsh reduction of benefits to those who make an extra effort to increase their earnings beyond some low minimum. Moreover, it increases the chance that the program would have politically active beneficiaries who press for good administration and high-quality services. It is likely that, as in France, broader coverage would create broader support for it.

Specifically, the Help for Working Parents program would contain the following provisions, many of which contain elements of the French child welfare system adapted to the U.S. institutional and political landscape:

1. Health insurance would be guaranteed to all families with children. This would mean providing access to health insurance and paying all of the cost for the poorest families and most of the cost for the rest.

2. Child care for preschool children and after-school care for older children would be provided free for lower-income families and would be subsidized for middle-income families. Specifically, the program proposed here would allow a 100 percent subsidy to those households that fall into the bottom 20 percent of families with children, and sliding-scale fees to families in the next two quintiles. The program would provide vouchers usable at private care facilities, including those affiliated with religious institutions. No parent would be forced to place a child in day care, but places would be provided for infants over the age of one month.

3. Income supplementation for low-wage families, through the Earned Income Tax Credit and food stamps would continue as currently on the books. Housing assistance, in the form of vouchers, would be provided to lower-income families with children in higher-rent areas as an entitlement.

4. The establishment and enforcement of child support orders would become a federal function, to be administered by the Internal Revenue Service (IRS). The amount to be paid would be a legislatively set proportion of the payee's current income.[15] All payments by absent parents would be made to the IRS, which would disburse them to the recipients. A program of child support assurance would be set up to benefit mothers who voluntarily help in establishing paternity, with the government guaranteeing a minimum monthly child support payment, even if less were collected.[16]

5. Parents who remain out of the labor force or who are between jobs would receive a combination of child support payments and vouchers for goods and services sufficient to bring the family up to the poverty line as defined by the BNB. For unemployed single parents who have failed to establish paternity, income support would consist mostly of vouchers—a "low-cash fallback."

Certain classes of single parent families will have to be covered by special programs: single parents who are students, those who are disabled, and those who are taking care of disabled children.

The Cost of Help for Working Parents   The cost of instituting the Help for Working Parents program would depend mainly on two factors: the number of parents moving into the labor market, and the number who would take advantage of the free or subsidized child care. Table 7.3 gives an estimate of the 1994 level of costs, assuming that about 60 percent of those currently on AFDC became labor force participants. (The realism of that assumption is discussed below.) The net additional cost is tallied at $86 billion per year, or $78 billion in 1991 magnitudes, an increase of 71 percent over the cost of the present system in that year.

TABLE 7.3 ESTIMATION OF COST FOR CURRENT PROGRAMS HELPING
LOW-INCOME FAMILIES WITH CHILDREN, VERSUS PROPOSED
HELP-FOR-WORKING-PARENTS (HWP) PROGRAM
(1994 MAGNITUDES)

	Current Program	HWP Program	Difference
Families without a parent in the labor force			
Number in millions	4.7	2.0	−2.7
	Billions of dollars		
AFDC	$25.3	—	−$25.3
Food stamps	11.5	4.9	−6.6
Job training for AFDC clients	1.0	—	−1.0
Housing assistance	6.0	10.2	+4.2
Medical care	24.3	10.3	−14.0
Child care	13.6	19.0	+5.4
Low-cash fallback	—	7.5	+7.5
Total, families with no parent in labor force	81.7	51.9	−29.8
Families with parent(s) in the labor force			
Number in millions	2.3	5.0	+2.7
	Billions of dollars		
EITC	$10.3	$22.5	+$12.1
Food stamps	2.2	4.7	+2.5
Housing assistance	3.4	7.3	+4.0
Medical care	10.3	53.6	+43.3
Child care	12.6	61.3	+48.7
Unemployment insurance	0.5	1.5	+1.0
Low-cash fallback	—	4.5	+4.5
Total, families with parent(s) in labor force	39.4	155.4	+116.1
Grand total	121.1	207.3	+86.3

Sources: Data on spending for current programs, including both federal and nonfederal expenditures, are based on the following sources: EITC cost is from U.S. Department of the Treasury, *Statistics of Income Bulletin* 12 (Spring 1993): 12. The child-care expenditures include spending for kindergartens, which are mostly half-day programs and which, under the HWP program, would be converted to full-day programs. Kindergarten spending was derived from material in National Center for Education Statistics, *Digest of Education Statistics, 1993* (Washington, 1993). The remainder derive from U.S. Bureau of the Census, *Statistical Abstract of the United States, 1993* (Washington, 1993) and Vee Burke, "Cash and Noncash Benefits for Persons with Limited Income: Eligibility Rules, Recipient and Expenditure Data, FY 1990–92," 93-382 EPW (Washington: Congressional Research Service, 1993). Distribution by family situation is in proportion to number of children under age eighteen in each category and data on program beneficiaries in U.S. Bureau of the Census, *Poverty in the United States: 1992,* Current Population Reports, Series P60-185 (Washington: U.S. Government Printing Office, 1993).

The bulk of the additional costs are, of course, for additional child-care and health-care benefits. The figures in the table do not reflect the effect of improved child support enforcement and child support assurance. There would be some saving on support now going to families with nobody in the labor force, as child support payments assumed a greater part of the burden of providing for the expenses of those not in jobs, but administrative costs would rise and the cost of the Earned Income Tax Credit might double as more families became eligible.

On balance, better child support flows would reduce public costs. The estimates in table 7.3 also do not reflect the modest addition that those new to the labor force would make to tax revenues.

If the government started to provide health care for those low-income workers who did not get it through their job, some other employers would stop providing it. This would accelerate the shedding of health care benefits by employers that is already occurring, and would bring nearer the day when the country would be forced to adopt a health care system that is not employment-based. However, in the course of this process, the cost to the government of

---

Notes to table 7.3: Estimates are based on 1991 magnitudes, escalated by 10 percent to approximate 1994 levels. The difference between the total for current programs in the first column of this table and the total of American expenditure reported in table 6.1 is accounted for by that escalation, and by $25.4 billion in tax breaks in the federal and state income taxes that are included as expenditures in table 6.1 but not in this table.

For the HWP program, Jean Kimmel suggests that the provision of child care, without the provision of health insurance, would cause a large shift of at-home mothers into the labor force. See Jean Kimmel, "Child Care Costs as a Barrier to Employment for Single and Married Mothers" (Kalamazoo, Mich.: W.E. Upjohn Institute for Employment Research, October 1994). It is assumed here that 60 percent of AFDC mothers would move into the labor force if both child care and health insurance were provided. It is assumed that the lowest quintile of families with children would get free child care, and that the next two quintiles would pay on a sliding scale. Children under six would get full-day care at $4,800 per year, and children ages six through twelve would get after-school and summer care at $3,600. Participation of 100 percent is assumed for families with working parents, 90 percent for others. The figures for medical care include funds to allow all families with children (regardless of income) not currently covered by health insurance to come under Medicaid. It is assumed that of those low-income families with a parent in the labor market, the unemployment rate would be 10 percent. Some unemployed would be eligible to receive unemployment insurance; others would be given the "low-cash fallback" package, which would provide vouchers for food, rent, transportation and utilities, and a small amount of cash. That package would also replace AFDC for out-of-the-labor-force families, and is assumed to cost the government on a per-family basis what AFDC plus food stamps cost, plus the cost of an increased set of housing benefits. For the latter families, food stamp and housing expenditures are shown separately. Savings to the government from the replacement of some AFDC payments by increased child support collections under a child support assurance program are not included in these estimates.

providing health insurance to uncovered families with children would grow.

The major benefits under the Help for Working Parents solution are similar to those in many existing state programs designed to wean people off welfare. These programs also provide health care and child care benefits, but only for a limited period, typically a year. They are restricted to a small fraction of those on welfare. The Help for Working Parents program differs from these programs in its far more ambitious aim—it is not restricted to getting people off welfare, although it is designed to accomplish that goal in a high proportion of cases. Its aim is to keep children, including those with job-holding parents who have never been on welfare, out of deprivation.

WHY HEALTH AND CHILD-CARE BENEFITS SHOULD BE PROVIDED IN KIND

Most economists have taken the position that government benefits to households are best given in the form of cash, rather than in the form of goods and services or vouchers. They reason that the government's dollars will provide their maximum utility if the family, rather than the taxpayers, chooses how to spend them. The program proposed here for families with children violates that "wisdom," since a high proportion of the proposed government expenditure would go to purchasing health care and child care.

Providing health insurance in the form of vouchers, rather than as a cash grant, is obviously the better way—so obviously better that it has not occurred even to the most orthodox economists to propose that the existing government and employer-provided programs be cashed out. It is worthwhile spelling out the reasons that this is the case, so that we can later see whether some of the same arguments can be applied to the provision of child care.

The families with children that concern us the most—those with low incomes—are those least likely to use their tight resources to purchase health care services. Unless visits to the physician are free or very cheap, these families may fail to get immunizations and other preventive care and may neglect minor complaints like sore throats that could turn into major problems if untreated. Moreover, children are not in a position to participate in the decision to buy care or not buy it, and may be permanently injured if their parents try to save money on medical care and guess wrong.

Clearly, the public has an interest in making sure that all parents can take their children and themselves to the physician for preventive care and sickness care without being deterred by the price. That means they have to have insurance, and the only way to make sure that a family has health insurance is to provide it to them on a free or highly subsidized basis. Some families in the United States who do not get health insurance from an employer or from the government do voluntarily buy it out of their own budget, but about half of those without insurance from employers or the government go without.[17] The reasons for that are varied. Currently in the United States, some families are unable to buy health insurance at any price on the private market. Some, on low budgets, may be able to buy it, but only at a price that would require a painful renunciation of goods they consider even more vital. Some, even out of an ample budget, may choose not to buy it, gambling that nobody in their family will need expensive treatment.

It is reasonable to regard prepaid health care as a "merit good," something that in our ethical judgment everybody should have, whether or not they are willing or able to buy it.[18] To ensure universal possession of a merit good means erecting a system of provision, rather than ensuring that everybody can afford the good in question. That is why medical care is provided as a service at government or employer expense, and not taken care of by a cash grant.

Some of the same arguments can be used to maintain that high-quality child care is also a merit good. If we insist that single parents hold a job, it can certainly be argued that the public has a strong interest in ensuring that children are well cared for while their parents work. To a greater extent even than medical care, we cannot stint on child care without chancing severe and permanent damage to our children. Moreover, children from all strata of society are arguably entitled to a safe, nurturing, and comfortable daytime environment—one that might otherwise be unavailable to poor children, and that high-quality out-of-home child care could provide. It could insulate them for most of their waking hours from dangerous neighborhoods, acculturate them to mainstream values and habits, and improve their readiness for school. In public facilities, or publicly regulated facilities, children can receive preventive health care, the diagnosis and remediation of health and emotional problems, nutritional meals, and attention to cognitive and behavioral development. There also would be a greater chance of detecting abuse.

We might try to force parents through law to place their children in licensed care, but such an "unfunded mandate" on poor parents would create intolerable hardship. High-quality child care, like medical care, is a major expenditure. Single mothers who buy child care were found to be spending 21 percent of their budget on their child-care bills.[19] Job-holding parents close to the poverty line could not buy high-quality care without sacrificing goods and services they feel they need even more. Many near-poor parents will be tempted to avoid buying high-quality care, in favor of a lower-cost alternative or zero-cost alternative that may end up damaging the child. It can be surmised that, like many of their higher-income counterparts, many or most single parents with incomes just sufficient to buy the goods and services specified in the BNB use or would use substandard child-care providers. A recent survey has indeed shown that much of the care currently being purchased by parents—middle class as well as poor—is substandard.[20] Providing high-quality child care through vouchers or the direct provision of services is the only way to ensure that the children actually receive it.

Therefore, just as with medical care, we should not provide an unearmarked cash benefit to cover child care. Aside from the quality assurance problem, the parent might use such a cash benefit for other living expenses that do not directly benefit the child and refrain from job holding, since the child-care benefit for two or more preschool children would be larger than the current welfare benefit. We could institute a job-holding requirement for those getting the benefit, but verification of job holding would be difficult. Moreover, from a political point of view, those who view single parents as irresponsible are more likely to favor benefits for direct services for the children. Also, shifting away from a cash benefit removes the suspicion that parents will have more children for the purpose of augmenting their cash benefit.

Free or highly subsidized high-quality child care would almost certainly increase the number of wives in two-parent families who take jobs, which some people would deplore. The subsidy could be denied or lowered for two-parent families, but this would be unfair, as well as an incentive for single parenthood.

COULD OR WOULD CURRENT
AFDC CLIENTS GET JOBS?

A major assumption of the Help for Working Parents solution is that a considerable number of the single mothers currently on welfare would get jobs. Two objections are commonly raised. One is that there are no jobs for them. Another is that large numbers of mothers currently on welfare could not hold a job without training. Both of these objections need examination and can be challenged.

In discussions of changing the welfare system, it is common to hear adherents of the "full welfare" solution say, "There are no jobs out there for those people." Nobody, however, says, "We can't allow the current crop of high school seniors to graduate because there are no jobs out there for them" or "Immigrants, legal or illegal, should know better than to come to the United States, because there are no jobs there for them." In fact, the number of jobs grows in most months, and people who enter the labor market compete for the vacancies that result from job growth and turnover. Most people who enter the labor force do not stay unemployed forever, even in periods of low growth. A 6 percent unemployment rate, together with a 3 percent monthly rate of turnover, implies that unemployment lasts, on average, for about two months, whether it results from losing or leaving a job or from entering the labor market for the first time.

In 1992, 3.7 million single mothers were living below the poverty line, of whom about 40 percent were employed for part of the year.[21] In that year, 9.4 million people were unemployed on average, and the unemployment rate averaged 7.4 percent.[22] If 60 percent of welfare mothers had in that year moved into the labor force seeking full-time, year-round work, and if the number of jobs did not increase as a result, the number of unemployed people would have risen by roughly two million, and the unemployment rate would have climbed to about 9.0 percent.[23] This would have increased the average spell of unemployment by about three weeks. Such an increase would certainly be undesirable, but it would not be enough to defeat the move from welfare to jobs.

In fact, a welfare reform based on the HWP concept would create new jobs. The provision of additional child care would create thousands of new jobs in child-care centers. The HWP would work best if jobs in public service employment were created in geographic areas with high unemployment rates, if illegal immigration were more effectively curbed, and if the hours that full-time high school students were permitted to work were legally curtailed. Nevertheless, some single mothers will have spells of unemployment and will need support during those periods. Better unemployment insurance coverage for single parents, and support for parents disabled from work, would also be needed. At present only 40 percent of the unemployed get unemployment insurance.[24]

As table 7.2 showed, jobs with no skill requirement besides an intelligence in the normal range—those paying the minimum wage—would suffice to get families with no more than two children up to the BNB standard, if child care and health care are provided. It is widely assumed that single mothers on welfare would need extensive training to be employable even in these jobs. For example, Robert Haveman speaks of "the extreme gaps between the capabilities of most existing welfare beneficiaries and the minimal cognitive and skill requirements of even the lowest-wage private jobs."[25] Yet, high school students and immigrants with little or no ability to speak English get and perform satisfactorily in such jobs by the millions without special government-financed training. While some single parents, particularly those with drug, alcohol, physical, or mental problems, may be inferior as workers to the general run of job-holding teenagers, there is no reason to think that most of them are.

Accordingly, the HWP budget allots no funds for training. By contrast, the welfare reform proposals of President Clinton, as well as those of his predecessors, allocated a considerable share of budgeted funds to job training. Unfortunately, these programs, on which tens of billions of dollars have been spent, seem to have had very little success in improving outcomes for the trainees.[26] Perhaps such programs would be more successful if the current system's disincentives to hold jobs were replaced by the incentives that the HWP system offers.

One pessimistic assessment of welfare mothers' employability is based on a study of the labor market experience of the former recipients of a Michigan general assistance (GA) program that was terminated in 1991.[27] Interviews two years later showed that of the former GA recipients who were high school dropouts, only 28 percent had jobs in the month of the survey, and of GA recipients who were high school graduates, only 46 percent had them. This experience does not necessarily forecast a low success rate for mothers on welfare who seek employment, if they could receive highly subsidized child care and health insurance, together with child support assurance.

Many of the GA recipients may well have had characteristics that made them particularly difficult to employ, and indeed one in four were able to get disability benefits after the termination of the GA program. Moreover, the GA program paid only $160 a month, providing those who lacked other sources of support with the most powerful possible incentive to get a job, even while the GA program continued. It is likely that many of those GA recipients remaining on the program who failed to respond to this incentive were relatively unemployable, so the failure of many of them to get and keep jobs when the program ended is not surprising.

Mothers on AFDC, on the other hand, have considerably higher cash and near-cash benefits than do GA recipients. They also get child care and health insurance benefits, which they lose if they leave the program. Thus AFDC recipients have little or no incentive to leave the program, which explains why many previous attempts to get them off welfare have failed. The establishment of such benefits under an HWP program should increase their incentive considerably. The ability of mothers on AFDC to find and keep jobs will get a realistic test only when their incentives to do so improve.

Some single mothers would certainly benefit from on-the-job training or apprenticeships in male-dominated crafts jobs (a type of training they seldom get in government-sponsored "jobs" programs), and others would benefit from going to college. Here, however, we run up against the kind of unfairness pointed out by Senator Gramm, quoted in chapter 6. Would it be fair to give parents on welfare an entitlement to such desirable things as training for blue-collar jobs and full college scholarships, while those who support themselves and their children in low-wage jobs would not be entitled to them? More subsidies for all lower-income people to get whatever training and education they need would be desirable, but it would add tens of billions of dollars to the annual budget. In crafting a program to drastically reduce child poverty, an expensive training and education component, while desirable, is not an indispensable component.

Even without the "push" of a time limit on welfare, the permanent guarantee of health insurance and the provision of child care—not just on a transitional basis but for as long as the children are of an age to require it (as done in France)—would greatly motivate mothers on welfare to take jobs. Without the huge financial drain of paying for child care and health care, an employed mother in a low-wage job would get to keep a far higher proportion of her paycheck.

The research of Spalter-Roth and Hartmann shows that many women who receive AFDC participate in the market for paid work. Of women who received AFDC benefits for at least two months out of a two-year period, 42 percent combined welfare and work, either sequentially or simultaneously. Some of their work was part-time or "off the books," which allowed them to keep their medical benefits.[28] Apparently, a good share of the welfare mothers will take paid work if it will improve their situation. Preliminary studies also suggest that mothers at home would voluntarily move into the labor force in great numbers if child care were available on a free or highly subsidized basis.[29]

HWP PROPOSAL VERSUS THE FRENCH SYSTEM

The $86 billion extra annual expenditure proposed here would make the HWP system about as expensive as the French system on a per capita basis and would finance a greatly expanded program in child care and health insurance that should suffice to lower poverty among children to a considerable degree. Not included is the provision of a universal child cash allowance of any size, which would add billions to the cost. The preference for including new child-care subsidies rather than a new child allowance is based on the likelihood that subsidized child care will encourage job holding. Moreover, the Earned Income Tax Credit, as currently authorized, partially fills the function of a child allowance. To summarize, the HWP system has a somewhat different profile from that of the French system:

Child care: For children under age three, the HWP system would pay for more care than the French system does, providing more care for the youngest children—those under three. This would keep many new single mothers in school or at work. On the other hand, the HWP system would not duplicate the French provision of free nursery schools for children above two-and-a-half to all income groups. Partial financing of child care would be available for 60 percent of all children, and only the bottom 20 percent would get full support.

Income support: The HWP system would not offer child allowances (or their tax-break equivalent) to families at all income levels. The current Earned Income Tax Credit and food stamp benefits, both of which are severely restricted to families with low income, would continue. The fallback grant to unemployed single mothers would improve, but would continue to be less generous than the French provision for this group. In France, the primary welfare-like program has a time limit, but those affected by it can move over to another program. Moreover, French officials have recourse to discretionary funds to help those whose eligibility for regular programs has expired. A time limit has not been specified for the HWP fallback grant.

Medical care: The HWP system would provide medical insurance to all families with children who do not receive it from an employer. France has universal medical insurance, covered by a payroll tax.

EVALUATING SIDE EFFECTS

In thinking about a change in American policy toward children, we have to consider the costs and side effects of whatever program design is followed. How does the proposed policy affect the incentive to take paid work and to form or refrain from forming single-parent families? What is the impact of such programs on teenagers, who, in addition to lacking material resources, may lack the maturity and the support necessary to nurture the children they might have?

Estimating the way a new program might affect parents' or prospective parents' behavior is far from an exact science. How and whether programs to aid single-parent families influence the rate of births outside of marriage is not clear. Conservatives suggest that withdrawing aid would largely eliminate such births, while the bulk of social science research suggests the opposite.[30] The extent to which a set of programs that increased the incentive to get a job—

as the program presented here would do—would increase the proportion of single parents in jobs is also something that cannot be estimated with any confidence. These uncertainties suggest that it would be wise to introduce new programs on a small-scale experimental basis, rather than rush into drastic changes on a large scale.

Beyond the technical problems of estimating a program's effects, we need to clarify our ethical feelings: the importance we attach to the various positive and negative effects of such a program, and whether we are willing to tolerate the negative effects in order to achieve the positive effects a policy promises. How much poverty among children are we willing to tolerate in order to discourage improvident childbearing or to penalize impecunious single parents who avoid paid work? How generous are we prepared to be in supporting with public resources the decision of any woman, regardless of age, economic circumstance, marital status, and number of previous births, to have a new baby? How attached are we to the idea that mothers may respectably and without social penalty choose to stay home with children, even if no private means of support are available, and those means must be provided out of the public purse?

✤ CHAPTER 8 ✤

Can We Conquer Child Poverty in America Through Political Action?

I
N THE NEAR TERM, there is little chance that the United States
will move toward a system for fighting child poverty modeled
on that of the French. That would require much greater expenditure and more federal administrative supervision. Rather, the
United States appears to be moving toward a system that puts
fewer resources into helping low-income families with children and
devolves administrative responsibility onto the states while keeping
the same basic pattern of the distribution of benefits—very little
help to parents in low-wage jobs. The incidence of poverty among
children in the United States has been rising, and these developments should accelerate that rise. However, unless the United
States is prepared to tolerate this worsening situation indefinitely,
some alternative program must eventually be tried. Therefore it is
worthwhile to compare the HWP with some of the alternative programs that have been proposed for the reduction of child poverty.

THE RECOMMENDATIONS OF THE NATIONAL COMMISSION ON CHILDREN

The National Commission on Children (NCC) was authorized by
federal legislation passed in 1987, with a mandate "to assess the status of children and families in the United States and propose new

directions for policy and program development ... [as well as] to design an action agenda for the 1990s and to build the necessary public commitment and sense of common purpose to see it implemented."[1] Two-thirds of the thirty-four members were selected by the Democratic leaders of the Congress, and one-third by the Republican president.

Members spanned the political spectrum. On the left were devoted advocates of government activism on behalf of poor children, who believe that the country is miserably failing large numbers of its children. On the right were fiscally and socially conservative members of the Bush administration, who blame the problems of poor American children on their parents' errant personal behavior, and who see the reform of that behavior as the only real solution to children's problems. Despite this diversity of opinion and orientation, the commission, whose report was issued in 1991, apparently tried for unanimity and achieved it on most issues. The desire to win approval for the report from the members at the far right end of the political spectrum must have limited severely what could be proposed; much of the report must be viewed as the result of a negotiated compromise.

The text of the commission's report presents the situation of poor children as a reproach to the nation: "If we measure success not just by how well most children do, but by how poorly some fare, America falls far short."[2] The commission presented a long list of policy recommendations, together with an accounting of their budgetary implications.

The most expensive item proposed—indeed, the only expensive item—was the equivalent of a child allowance of $1,000 per year for each child, paid to all parents regardless of income. The commission proposed a refundable tax credit in that amount, which would result in a cash payment to low-income families who owe little or no tax, and a reduction in the income tax owed by the rest. It would be partly financed by the repeal of the personal exemption for children, which benefits only those families with enough income to be subject to income tax, and benefits those in the upper brackets more than those in the lower brackets. The commission estimated the cost of the tax credit to the Treasury at an additional $40 billion per year. The commission also backed a system of child support assurance—better collection of child support payments from absent parents, with a guaranteed government-provided minimum payment to the resident parent if the absent parent is remiss.

A majority of the commission felt that the country should take steps to ensure that all children and pregnant women are covered by health insurance, although it fell short of proposing a simple government-financed program to accomplish that. Instead, it proposed requiring employers either to cover insurance for employees' children and pregnant, unemployed spouses or to pay a tax that would help to finance government provision.[3] Subsidized public coverage was advocated for those children and pregnant women who could not be covered through employment-related benefits. Reforms of exclusionary insurance-industry practices and cost-control measures were also advocated. The commission estimated that its health package would entail only $7.4 billion in additional federal spending, plus an $8.7 billion expenditure by currently non-insuring employers. These recommendations on health care, which did not include coverage of nonpregnant women, drew dissents from most of the Republican members of the commission.[4]

The commission gave lip service to the importance of child care, endorsing "such additional [federal] funding as is necessary to ensure that high-quality child care services are available to all children and families that need them."[5] However, its report gives evidence of a reluctance to tackle the issue realistically. In its discussion of the difficult transition from welfare to work, the report lists only $1,250 as the annual "work expenses" faced by a single mother with two children who is moving into full-time work.[6] This is perhaps 13 percent of the cost of high-quality child care for the children if they are both under school age.

The commission's report called for steadily rising federal expenditures for child care, starting at an additional $143 million in fiscal 1992, rising to $552 million additional in 1996. However, compared with the amounts allocated to child care in the HWP program, the commission's allocations represent a fraction of the sums needed to provide high-quality care to those going from welfare to work. It would provide nothing for working families who are poor and near poor, and nothing for any subsidies to the less affluent sections of the middle class.

A more activist stance on child care in the report would undoubtedly have met more explicit dissent by the Republican appointees to the commission. Evidence of revolt against even the modest and vague recommendations in this area appears in the letter that Commissioner Gerald (Jerry) P. Regier wrote for inclusion in the report volume. After calling for the elimination of AFDC, he says,

> *I continue to object to an increase in government-financed child-care programs.* This is for fiscal reasons as well as concern for the potential negative effects upon children, especially infants and preschoolers. Attachment of young children to their parents is critical to healthy development, and the research is beginning to make a connection to present high-risk activities of youth. We should take these warning signs seriously and lean toward promoting more direct parental care. (Emphasis in original.)[7]

Regier did not address the contradiction between his attitudes on AFDC and child care, a contradiction common among conservatives.

The commission did endorse full funding for the Head Start program, which, since it does nothing to help with custodial care, is apparently not seen on the right as contravening the principle that a mother should care for her child full time.[8] The commission was eloquent in support of a broad range of other services to help families with children, but it recommended that only $2.6 billion in additional federal money be spent under seventeen other program categories.

The major difference between the agendas supported by the National Commission on Children and that of the Help for Working Parents system is, of course, that the NCC supported an additional cash benefit while the HWP supports using the expenditure for the provision of child care. The NCC would spend $40 billion on a $1,000 grant per child per year. The HWP would spend $54 billion on child care. The NCC benefit would go equally to parents in all income groups; the child-care benefit of the HWP would go to the lower 60 percent of families, but give most help to those in the bottom quintile of the income scale. Both the NCC and the HWP proposals would put all children under health insurance; the latter would also guarantee health insurance to their parents.

The NCC plan would be less effective than the HWP plan in increasing the attractiveness of work over welfare, because the HWP plan would remove the need to pay out a high proportion of wage income for child care. The tax credit, which would add cash equally to existing welfare grants and to wages, would raise the standard of living of those on welfare and those at work.[9] Thus, it would contribute little if anything to the relative attractiveness of work over welfare. With the tax credit, the family would be in a better position to pay for child care, but steep child-care costs would continue to be a major deterrent to taking a job. For a family with two preschool children, child-care costs could exceed the tax credit by $7,500.

It is remarkable (and a tribute to the commission) that despite their diverse political leanings, the commissioners were able to maintain unanimity on most policy issues and that all joined to express the belief that the urgent situation of America's children required strong government action. However, no one rushed to enact the recommendations of the unanimous NCC report. The Republican administration was hostile to almost all of them, and the Democratic-controlled Congress had other preoccupations. By the time of the 1992 presidential campaign, both Republicans and Democrats were talking up a welfare reform that would treat single parents with greater severity. Overt attention to the reduction of poverty among children as a major goal for the nation had receded.

President Clinton never formally connected himself to the NCC's agenda. However, with little national attention, a rise in the Earned Income Tax Credit (EITC) to a maximum of $3,560 was enacted in his first year. With that, the NCC's general aim of bigger cash benefits to families with children was advanced. However, the benefit increase went only to the bottom part of the income distribution, and only to families with a parent in a paid job. Needless to add, had Clinton's attempt to achieve universal health insurance coverage succeeded, another major step recommended by the NCC would have been achieved.

THE CHILDREN'S DEFENSE FUND'S PROPOSALS

The Children's Defense Fund (CDF), a well-known and well-respected advocacy group located in Washington, D.C., has been a leader in lobbying the executive branch and Congress on behalf of poor children. Its publications document the high and rising rate of poverty among the country's children, assess the causes, and warn of the consequences.[10] The president of the CDF, Marian Wright Edelman, served on the National Commission on Children, and throughout the early 1990s the CDF's proposed agenda was broadly similar to the NCC's, with a number of additions. A leading component of its policy agenda in those years was a somewhat more generous version of the NCC's refundable tax credit, a grant of $1,200 to $1,300 per family member younger than eighteen, without regard to income. It has favored child support assurance. Unlike the NCC, it urged that AFDC stipends be made more generous, although it has acknowledged the AFDC's drawbacks in discouraging labor market participation.[11]

More strongly than the NCC, the CDF has emphasized labor market policies that would enhance the employability of young parents and improve and maintain their incomes—skill training programs, the creation of public sector jobs, raising the minimum wage, and improving the coverage of the unemployment insurance system.[12] The CDF's analysis of how an unfavorable labor market increases child poverty is undoubtedly correct, and all of its labor market suggestions are constructive.

However, the CDF's advocacy can contribute relatively little to the herculean task of improving the American labor market. More to the point is its advocacy of specific policies to boost resources to poor families in ways that improve the incentives and abilities of parents to seek jobs. The increase in the Earned Income Tax Credit in 1993 was a notable victory of this type.

Over the years, the CDF has embraced what it no doubt viewed as a realistic strategy of pushing for modest expansions in government help to families with children in a large number of disparate programs. It led the fight for a federal program in the child-care area and supported expanded government help with child care and medical insurance, which are the two main ingredients of the Help for Working Parents program. However, the CDF never suggested a program that it could claim was sufficient to drastically reduce child poverty.[13] It has not responded to the country's obvious desire to increase job holding among single parents, and it never came up with a "welfare reform" that would reduce child poverty while encouraging and enabling parents to work. Democrats in the Congress might have embraced such a plan, instead of the punitive Republican "reform," for which many of them felt obliged to vote in the absence of an alternative of this sort.

The election of November 1994, which brought to power a Republican party that had vowed to cut drastically the public resources going to poor parents and thus to poor children, has at least for a time closed the door on even the marginal improvements that the CDF advocated. The Children's Defense Fund, while fighting on a day-to-day basis to save the bits and pieces that it can, might during this difficult period consider the formulation of a bolder long-run policy, to serve as a rallying point when the political climate turns friendlier.

REDUCING CHILD POVERTY THROUGH IMPROVING LABOR MARKET OUTCOMES

Some observers suggest that the way to cure the child poverty problem is to increase the reward to low-skilled labor, rather than giving child care and health care services to families with children. Robert Haveman, for example, suggests wage rate subsidies that would halve the difference between the amount a person earns and a "target" of $8 an hour.[14] Those earning less than $8 an hour would have gross incomes of less than $16,640 a year, which, as we have seen, is not enough to allow a single mother to support two preschool children at a decent standard while paying for good child care.

Haveman may assume that, thanks to the better labor market outcome for low-skilled men that his proposal would bring, the proportion of children living in two-parent families would rise considerably, and the married mothers could stay home with their children. However, a resulting increase in marriage is far from a certainty. Men are, with increasing frequency, remaining bachelors, divorcing wives, and siring children outside of marriage.[15] Improving job availability and wages (beyond the improvement wrought by the Earned Income Tax Credit) would be desirable, might improve marriage rates somewhat, and would decrease child poverty. But we cannot assume that higher wages to men would dramatically change their social behavior and that enough benefits would trickle down from men to women to children to make a big dent in child poverty. The HWP program, by contrast, gives major resources directly to the families who need them most, in a form that is tailor-made to meet the needs of children.

"CUT 'EM OFF!": THE PROPOSAL OF THE RADICAL RIGHT

The idea that aid to poor families with children does more harm than good and should be discontinued has been adopted by a faction devoted to the ideas of Charles Murray. Starting in 1984, Mur-

ray has promoted the idea that the AFDC program, far from reliev-
ing the misery of the poor, has made it worse by enabling and
therefore promoting births to single parents and abstention from
work.[16] Many on the religious right are concerned with what they
see as the immorality of those on welfare: failure of the unmarried
to avoid sex and births. Murray professes to believe that abolishing
welfare would significantly reduce the number of children needing
taxpayers' support. However, he acknowledges that, at least in the
beginning, some parents could not or would not support their children by working for wages. His solution is to establish orphanages
for the children of destitute mothers.

The cost (or saving) to the government purse of Murray's suggested policy has never been estimated, perhaps because the policy
has not been considered a realistic possibility, even by its support-
ers.[17] Rather than a serious suggestion for policy, Murray's writings
may represent nothing more than his hostility toward an "under-
class" seen as expensive and prone to criminality, and one that has
made large cities uninhabitable by middle-class people. When the
Republicans, led by Newt Gingrich, won majority status in the U.S.
Congress in 1994, they ran on a platform that included Murray's
ideas of refusing welfare to certain categories of single mothers.

Very soon after the Congress convened, however, the Murray-
type aspects of the Republican plan were deemphasized. Instead,
the Republicans advocated that federal funds spent on welfare programs—AFDC, food stamps, Medicaid, school lunches—be dis-
persed to the states. The state governments would have considerable discretion in managing welfare and allied programs within
their borders. Moreover, the "entitlement" feature of AFDC, the
guarantee that every eligible family would get the benefits specified
by law, would come to an end.

If responsibility for the support of families with children is
devolved upon the states, they are likely to continue the AFDC-
type policy of concentrating help on mothers who stay home, with
little or no help to mothers in jobs. That is the cheapest policy for
keeping mothers and children out of destitution and homelessness.
Although the general outlines of the policy seem unlikely to change,
the level of support for mothers on welfare will probably shrink still
further. All of the states are in competition to lower taxes so as to
attract business and rich residents. Reducing the number of people
on welfare and reducing the benefit levels would help them to do

that. So state management of welfare would probably result in an erosion of benefits, and a greater hardship on poor children.

LONG-RUN PROSPECTS FOR A SERIOUS ATTACK ON CHILD POVERTY

The problem (and the disgrace) of poverty among America's children will not yield to the policy steps that are likely to be taken in the next few years. A policy likely to make serious inroads on child poverty, whether or not it is modelled on that of France, would require a large increase in the resources devoted to raising children, which must come in the form of government expenditures. It has been argued here that many of those resources would best be provided in the form of child care and health services. American politics moves in cycles, and there will inevitably come a time when Americans feel friendlier toward government activism than it does today. At that time, such activist programs might garner sufficient support to be judged worth the billions in extra public money they would cost. The proposals in this book have been presented with that time in mind.

Providing Health Care

In 1993–94, President Clinton attempted to establish universal health insurance in the belief that a substantial majority of the citizens supported it. He did not model his proposal on that of Canada, France, or any of the other countries providing universal coverage. The White House's plan was designed to reassure those people who were satisfied with their current arrangements that they could stay with them and with the physicians they trusted. Nevertheless, opponents to the president's plan for gaining universal coverage and instituting cost control succeeded in convincing such people that they would lose their freedom to choose their medical providers and to finance the medical care they wanted. The business community fought hard against a proposal that would have required them to cover all employees. The medical insurance industry also opposed the proposal. The complexity of the president's proposed program made it vulnerable to the charge that it was unworkable and that an incompetent government would complicate and destroy a system that was working tolerably well.

Despite the resounding defeat of the effort to achieve universal coverage, the unsatisfactory conditions that called the effort into being remain. The number of people uncovered will continue to increase, as employers seek to reduce the cost of employing people. Other efforts to move toward universal access to health care, and to rationalize the financial system paying for it, will clearly occur in the future. It would be desirable if the provision of health care for children and their families could be part of an overall plan of health services for the entire nation. On the other hand, universal access to health care may have to be achieved by stages, as universal access to government old-age pensions was. Medicare and Medicaid can be thought of as the first two stages. Current efforts to rein in the growth in their costs may increase the possibilities of adding new groups to coverage. The guarantee to children still uncovered, or to children and their families, may be an attractive next step with which to carry forward the move toward a universal system.

Providing Child Care

The political difficulty of substantially increasing the government's role in providing child care, one of the main features of the French system, will probably be greater than the difficulty of providing medical insurance. Few people have ideological objections to the proposition that people should have the right to go to the doctor. In the matter of paid child care, as we have seen, some have ideological objections even to its private purchase, and even more vociferous objections to any public subsidy. Some are opposed to non-mother care because they want women to care for their own children at home and stop competing with men for jobs.[18]

As previous chapters have stated, however, research shows that good-quality care can produce good results. Two factors will strengthen the hand of those pushing for government help in the child-care area. One is the high proportion of married women with children under age six who participate in the labor force (59 percent of white married women and 71 percent of black married women in 1993).[19] With a skillful and energetic leadership, so far missing, they and their families might be mobilized to support such help. The other is the increasing consensus on both the right and the left that single mothers should be earners, meaning that most of their children must be put into paid care. The inconsistency of the demands on the Right that welfare be ended and that at the same time all children should be cared for full-time by their mothers makes such a stand vulnerable to attack.[20]

It is not clear how the recently released evidence of substandard quality in many U.S. child-care facilities will affect the argument about the government's role in child care. On the one hand, it will strengthen those who say that out-of-home child care is to be avoided. On the other hand, since a mass return to at-home care is an unlikely response to this evidence, it may be taken as demonstrating the need for higher government licensing standards, more rigorous inspection, and more government financial support to centers.[21]

CONCERNS ABOUT THE GOVERNMENT'S ABILITY TO MANAGE AN EFFECTIVE PROGRAM

One difficulty in persuading the public to mount a large-scale program to fight child poverty is the widespread doubt that American governmental entities are capable of delivering high-quality services to children or managing the purchase of such services from private providers. While French voters appear to have a well-founded confidence in the ability of their civil servants, American voters do not have a like confidence in theirs.

Curing the problems of poor and near-poor children in the United States is a complicated task, on which the country has hardly made a start. These children and their communities have especially difficult problems and need public services that are organized to deal with them in an efficacious way. Children from lower-income families, more urgently than more fortunately situated children, need good-quality schools, which are difficult to provide in unruly neighborhoods, where many of the pupils themselves present discipline problems. They need safety from violence, which requires better acculturation of children to society's norms, as well as better policing, jurisprudence, and correctional systems. They need to be living with parents or other adults who are not incapacitated because of drug addiction, alcoholism, mental illness, or old age. In cases of neglect or abuse, they need prompt detection and rescue by public social service agencies. They need a medical system that can deliver preventive care and that is organized to powerfully motivate parents to take advantage of such care. None of that is in prospect.

Organizing educational, medical, police, and social services to provide for such needs requires public agencies to skillfully plan, experiment and execute programs that deliver services. Perhaps a new corps of civil servants is needed to organize this kind of service—one that could carry on small-scale experiments, and then replicate the successes and terminate the failures.

CAN WE AFFORD IT?

Another crucial roadblock in the way of a large-scale government program to reduce child poverty is the idea that, given the current budgetary situation, the United States cannot afford to spend more on social welfare programs, even those that would be of high value.[22] But "cannot afford" has two quite different meanings: it can mean literally financially impossible or imprudent, or it can mean that the desire to purchase the item in question is not strong enough to warrant restructuring one's budget.

A program that would provide child care and health insurance for lower- and middle-income families could be financed by a modest rearrangement of the budget. When the politicians are saying (and the citizens are echoing) that we "cannot afford" to spend more on such programs, they are playing a word game—pretending to use the phrase in its "imprudence" sense, rather than in its "insufficient desire" sense. No politician wants to say that we have better things to do with our resources than mobilizing them to improve child welfare in this country (through higher taxes, or reducing other expenditures, or borrowing). By all measures, the United States is an extremely wealthy country, and one of the least taxed in the developed world. Saying that we "cannot afford" the programs simply rings hollow in light of our country's vast resources.

The example of France, a country very like ours, and with somewhat fewer resources than we have at our disposal, shows that the "can't afford it" rationale for continuing to tolerate widespread child poverty is one that deserves questioning. Certainly, it is possible that the French programs, and the heavy taxes that support them, detract somewhat from economic performance and raise unemployment rates. Nevertheless, the French example should prompt us to ask whether it would be worth sacrificing some aspects of high economic performance in favor of reducing the child poverty rate approaching one in four to a rate of one in eighteen, as the French have done.[23]

A costly and activist program is the only way we will be able to make progress against child poverty. We cannot create, through government policy or moral suasion or religious revival, a society in which single mothers and their children will not need some help. We are unlikely to move anytime soon to a situation where all or almost all children are born to married couples, where almost all marriages last until death, and where all children have parents who earn enough to support them adequately. Such an alternative is closed to us, at least as the expected outcome of any series of actions by the government. If we are to make a serious attempt to design a government program to rescue millions of poor children whose predicament "cannot be countenanced by a wealthy nation, a caring people, or a prudent society," we must choose from the alternatives that are available to us. The passage of such a program must await the time when we have a president who can effectively frame and forward the required agenda, a time when generosity toward the "have-nots" is greater, and when antigovernment rhetoric has been overcome by an even more obvious need for action.

✣ NOTES ✣

PART I: TWO COUNTRIES, TWO RESPONSES

Chapter 1. How Two Countries Respond to Children's Needs

1. U.S. Bureau of the Census, *Income, Poverty, and Valuation of Non-cash Benefits, 1993*, Current Population Reports, Series P-60, No. 188 (Washington: U.S. Government Printing Office, 1995). See chapter 7 and the appendix for a discussion of the failure of the official poverty line to properly account for the expenses of working poor families.

2. National Commission on Children, *Beyond Rhetoric: A New American Agenda for Children and Families* (Washington: National Commission on Children, 1991), 3–4.

3. The programs in question are Medicaid, the Earned Income Tax Credit, and the Child Care and Development Block Grant. See the description of these programs in chapter 6.

4. See *Family Policy: Government and Families in Fourteen Countries*, ed. Sheila B. Kamerman and Alfred J. Khan (New York: Columbia University Press, 1978).

5. See Jonathan Bradshaw, John Ditch, Hilary Holmes, and Peter Whiteford, *Support for Children: A Comparison of Arrangements in Fifteen Countries* (London: Her Majesty's Stationery Office, 1993); *Digest of Statistics on Social Protection in Europe. Volume 4: Family* (Luxembourg: Office for Official Publications of the European Communities, 1993); Organisation for Economic Co-operation and Development (OECD), *Financing and Delivering Health Care: A Comparative Analysis of OECD Countries*, OECD Policy Studies, No. 4 (Paris: OECD, 1987); id., *Child Care in OECD Countries* (Paris: OECD, 1990). See, also, *Child Care, Parental Leave, and the Under 3s: Policy Innovation in Europe*, ed. by Sheila B. Kamerman and Alfred J. Kahn (New York: Auburn Imprint of Greenwood Publishing Group, 1991).

6. Timothy M. Smeeding, "Why the U.S. Antipoverty System Doesn't Work Very Well," *Challenge* 35 (January/February 1992): 30–35.

7. For analysis of the effect of Swedish policies, see Markus Jäntti and Sheldon Danziger, "Child Poverty in Sweden and the United States: The Effect of Social Transfers and Parental Labor Force Participation," *Industrial and Labor Relations Review* 48 (October 1994): 48–64.

8. For totals of French and American expenditures, see table 2.1 below, which summarizes the more detailed tables of chapters 3 through 6. For citations of the sources of the component expenditures, see the detailed tables in those chapters.

153

9. For a discussion of French pronatalism, see Susan Pedersen, *Family, Dependence, and the Origins of the Welfare State: Britain and France, 1914–1945* (New York: Cambridge University Press, 1993). See, also, Alisa Klaus, *Every Child a Lion: The Origins of Maternal and Infant Policy in the United States and France, 1890–1920* (Ithaca, N.Y.: Cornell University Press, 1993).

10. Only 13 percent of married couples surveyed in France in 1989 reported having more than two children, although some will go on to have additional children. See *Contours et caractères; les femmes* (Paris: Institut National de la Statistique et des Études Économiques, 1991), 41. The lifetime fertility rate for women is 1.82, which is less than the replacement rate but considerably higher than the fertility rates of most other countries of Western Europe (*Contours et caractères*, 35). French government officials are not above comforting themselves with the fact that the French birthrate now exceeds that of the Germans, who provide little help with child care, and whose school hours and shopping hours make it extremely difficult for mothers to hold jobs.

11. An article in the *New York Times* comments on the "strong national pride" of the French and the perception of their culture as a "vital part of the national identity." See Marlise Simons, "France to Form New Body to Further Protect Culture," *New York Times*, 25 February 1996, A:12.

12. Smeeding, "Why the U.S. Antipoverty System Doesn't Work Very Well."

Chapter 2. Differences in Spending and Program Design

1. These benefits are in the form of the Earned Income Tax Credit, a grant camouflaged as a tax break, and food stamps. See chapter 6 for a description. The minimum wage specified in the text is that set in 1991, and unchanged through 1995.

2. Sandra Hofferth, April Brayfield, Sharon Deich, and Pamela Holcomb, *National Child Care Survey, 1990* (Washington: Urban Institute, 1991), 178.

3. In 1991, 133,000 single parents were getting benefits under the *Allocation de Parent Isolé* (API) program, and 101,000 under the *Revenu Minimum d'Insertion* (RMI) program. In addition, the RMI program supported 77,000 couples with children. See chapter 4 for discussions of these programs. Of single mothers (and 1,541 single fathers) receiving the first-line French welfare-like benefit (API), only 37,435 did not have a child under three years of age. See *CAF statistiques; prestations familiales, 1991* (Paris: Caisse Nationale des Allocations Familiales, 1991), 252. For information on the number of French single mothers, see *Contours et caractères; les femmes* (Paris: Institut National de la Statistique et des Études Économiques, 1991), 40.

4. For U.S. figures, U.S. Bureau of the Census, *Statistical Abstract of the United States, 1993* (Washington, 1993) 59, 381. Of American welfare recipients, 33 percent had no children under age six.

5. For the magnitude of these expenditures and the sources of the data, see table 4.1 below.

6. Unemployment or nonparticipation in the labor market for as long as a year can result in the loss of health insurance obtained through participation in the social security system. However, many of the people in these circumstances receive health insurance through the RMI program described in chapter 4.

7. *Statistical Abstract of the United States, 1994* (Washington, 1994): 118. The percentage of those with privately provided coverage dropped steadily between 1987, when it was 75.5 percent, and 1992.

8. See *Economic Report of the President, Transmitted to the Congress February 1994* (Washington, 1994): 122–27.

9. U.S. Bureau of the Census, *Statistical Abstract of the United States, 1994*, 118.

10. Both countries spend large sums for public school grades one through twelve; the United States spent $199 billion in 1991 for public primary and secondary schools, while France spent 251 billion francs (the equivalent of spending $178 billion in a country the size of the United States). See Ministère de l'Éducation Nationale et de la Culture, *Repères et references statistiques sur les enseignements et la formation* (Paris, 1992), 213; and National Center for Education Statistics, *Digest of Education Statistics 1993* (Washington, 1993), 155.

11. Many of the public schools that serve mainly poor children in the United States are notoriously bad, and this obviously affects the quality of the children's lives for the worst while they attend them, and their income-earning potential when they become adults. See Jonathan Kozol, *Death at an Early Age: The Destruction of the Hearts and Minds of Negro Children in the Boston Public Schools* (Boston: Houghton Mifflin, 1967). While I do not focus on the matter in this book, such schools need drastic improvement, and most probably need additional expenditure.

12. The exchange rate designed to perform such a conversion, based on average prices for goods and services in the two countries, is called the "purchasing power parity" rate, which in 1991 was 6.51 francs per dollar. The rates are published by the Organisation for Economic Co-operation and Development. See *OECD in Figures* (Paris: OECD, 1993). The market exchange rate, which averaged 5.45 francs to the dollar in 1991, is of importance to importers, exporters, and tourists, but is less relevant to the budget comparisons made here. The latter rate is affected by imports and exports in the two countries, and by speculation about the future value of these currencies, while most of the benefits with which we are dealing involve goods and services produced within each country. A special purchasing

power parity rate was used for medical care expenditures (3.57 francs per dollar in 1991) because the cost of medical services is much higher relative to the cost of other goods and services in the United States than it is in France. Conversion of francs spent on medical care into dollars of equivalent purchasing power was based on material in *Health Systems* (Paris: OECD, 1993), 2: 66.

13. Meaningful comparison of spending in the two countries is easier when considering child care and income supplementation than medical care, since the United States does not provide national health insurance to its citizens, and France does. For the middle- and upper-income groups, employer-provided health insurance in the United States covers most of the needs that government-provided insurance covers in France. For spending on behalf of the lower parts of the income distribution—where, in the United States, public provision is concentrated—the comparison is still somewhat problematical, although less so. In table 2.1, France's medical care expenditures include national health insurance for families with children who are in the bottom quarter of the income distribution, as well as government expenditures on programs for preventive health care for children. The American expenditures on medical care shown in table 2.1 include Medicaid for low-income families with children.

14. I use the term "government spending" to include the expenditure on any benefit or activity mandated by public authority, central or local. By contrast, the French usually reserve the term "government" for the central authority, *l'État*. They do not count adjunct national institutions, such as the social security system, or the activities of departmental and local authorities, as part of "government." The various French benefits described in the text are routed through a large variety of public, semi-public, and private entities. Some are controlled by central government, and others by the *collectivités territoriales*, which include the *départements* and *collectivités locales*, corresponding roughly to states and localities in the United States. Some of the benefits sent to families with children are routed through nongovernmental bodies that are regulated by government entities. For example, some benefits are paid by "contributions" rather than by taxes, administered jointly by employers' and workers' unions. These are counted here as "government benefits" if they form part of a national system mandated by public authority.

15. Gilbert Steiner, a wry and knowledgeable observer of social policy debates, accused American child-care advocates of putting up a smoke screen when they proclaimed a "children's policy agenda" that included government provision of child care. What the child-care advocates were really after, Steiner said, was women's freedom to take jobs and to escape child care themselves. Steiner's target was middle-class married women, not poor single mothers. See Gilbert Y. Steiner with Pauline H. Milius, *The Children's Cause* (Washington: Brookings Institution, 1976). Steiner also considered the use of

the label "family policy" to be equally misleading, as in such influential works as *Family Policy: Government and Families in Fourteen Countries*, ed. Sheila B. Kamerman and Alfred J. Kahn (New York: Columbia University Press, 1978). Steiner viewed the use of the "family policy" label as an attempt to hijack the widespread approval of the traditional two-parent family. In *The Futility of Family Policy* (Washington: Brookings Institution, 1980), Steiner says that those who appropriate "family policy" in such a way are using that approval to advance measures that many would otherwise find unacceptable.

16. This is the way that Senator Phil Gramm, Republican senator from Texas and former presidential candidate for the 1996 election, frequently describes them.

17. Charles Murray, *Losing Ground: American Social Policy, 1950–1980* (New York: Basic Books, 1984).

18. See, for example, Penelope Leach, *Children First* (New York: Alfred A. Knopf, 1994).

19. See discussion of this issue in chapter 6.

20. Murray, *Losing Ground*.

PART II: FRENCH PROGRAMS FOR CHILD WELL-BEING

Chapter 3. Government Child-Care Programs in France

1. Some of the costs in table 3.1, particularly those for before-and-after-school care and summer camps, are estimated indirectly by using total expenditures and client data.

2. *Contours et caractères; les enfants de moins de 6 ans* (Paris: Institut National de la Statistique et des Études Économiques, 1992), 75.

3. Ministère de l'Éducation Nationale et de la Culture, *Repères et références statistiques sur les enseignements et la formation* (Paris, 1992), 165.

4. Ministère de l'Éducation Nationale, *L'école maternelle: son rôle/ses missions* (Paris: Centre National de Documentation Pédagogique, 1986).

5. Any shortage of places is concentrated in the two- to three-year-old group by making them wait for admission.

6. See Ministère de l'Éducation Nationale, *L'école maternelle: son rôle/ses missions*.

7. Alain Norvez, *De la naissance à l'école* (Évry: Institut National d'Études Démographiques et Presses Universitaires de France, 1990), 386.

8. *Repères et références statistiques sur les enseignements et la formation* (1992), 13.

9. France leads all of the OECD countries in the extent to which its young children attend nursery school. See Organisation for Economic Co-operation and Development, *Child Care in OECD Countries* (Paris: OECD, 1990), 14.

10. For a description of these services, see below.

11. Carollee Howes and Elizabeth Marx, "Raising Questions about Improving the Quality of Child Care: Child Care in the United States and France," *Early Childhood Research Quarterly* 7 (1992): 347–66.

12. *Cost, Quality & Child Outcomes in Child Care Centers, Executive Summary*, second edition, ed. Suzanne Helburn (Denver, Economics Department, University of Colorado at Denver, 1995): 17.

13. This is the number quoted at the Ministry of Education. Carollee Howes and Elizabeth Marx report observing an average of 22. Howes and Marx, "Raising Questions about Improving the Quality of Child Care": 353.

14. Gail Richardson and Elizabeth Marx, *A Welcome for Every Child: How France Achieves Quality in Child Care* (New York: The French-American Foundation, 1989).

15. See A. Atkinson, "French Preprimary Education: A Tradition of Responding to Children," *Early Child Development and Care* 46 (1989): 77–86. See, also, Howes and Marx, "Raising Questions about Improving the Quality of Child Care."

16. Howes and Marx, "Raising Questions about Improving the Quality of Child Care."

17. The maximum annual housing allowance for teachers who do not get free housing is 12,000 francs ($1,478).

18. Information provided by Vincent Poubelle and Michel Grignon of the Caisse Nationale des Allocations Familiales.

19. See Myra H. Strober, Suzanne Gerlach-Downie, and Kenneth E. Yeager, "Child Care Centers as Workplaces," *Feminist Economics* 1 (Spring 1995): 93–120.

20. Ministère de l'Éducation Nationale et de la Culture, "Le coût de l'éducation," Note d'Information 92.20 (Paris, 1992). Some government money is spent on schools not under public management, so the per-pupil expenditure rate for the public facilities is lower than the total spent divided by the number of children served by the public system.

21. Clifford and Russell give a figure of $5,000 for high quality care in the late 1980's, while the Cost, Quality, and Child Outcomes Study done in 1993 found the average cost of care to be $4,940 in the states it studied. See R. Clifford and S. Russell, "Financing Programs for Pre-school-aged Children," *Theory into Practice*, 28(1) (Winter 1989): 19–27, and *Cost, Quality, and Child Outcomes in Child Care Centers*.

22. Norvez, *De la naissance à l'école*, 398.

23. The policies concerning an institution of such importance are quite naturally a subject of continuing controversy. See Christine Garin

and Martine Valo, "La maternelle en danger," *Le monde de l'éducation* (September 1990): 20–39.

24. These data need to be interpreted with caution. Those children with little or no experience in nursery school are likely to be those with physical or mental disabilities or recent immigrants. Thus, it would probably not be correct to attribute their relatively poor showing in first grade entirely to their lack of attendance at nursery school.

25. For information on France's ethnic minorities, see Organisation for Economic Co-operation and Development, *OECD in Figures* (Paris: OECD, 1990).

26. *Repères et références statistiques sur les enseignements et la formation* (1990), 107.

27. The one exception is the *Revenue Minimum d'Insertion*, which is a welfare-like benefit for the long-term unemployed, with or without children. Recent immigrants do not receive the RMI. See the discussion of this benefit in chapter 4.

28. For an account of this incident, see Steven Greenhouse, "For Emigres, A Lesson that Begins in the Nursery," *New York Times* 3 March 1990, p. 10.

29. This is well illustrated by the Ministry of Education's ban on the head scarves that some Muslim girls and women have worn. The Education Minister, in announcing the ban on the scarves, said, "The will of our people was to build a united, secular society, particularly where schools were concerned ... We cannot accept ostentatious signs that divide our youth." See Youssef M. Ibrahim, "France Bans Muslim Scarf in Its Schools," *New York Times*, 11 September 1994, p. 4.

30. A 1993 survey showed annual turnover rates of 36 percent. In some for-profit centers the turnover rates were above 50 percent. See *Cost, Quality, and Child Outcomes in Child Care Centers, Technical Report*, ed. by Suzanne W. Helburn (Denver: Department of Economics, University of Colorado at Denver, 1995). For turnover rates and the correlation between turnover and quality of care, see tables 5.11 and 13.3, respectively.

31. See *Contours et caractères; les enfants de moins de 6 ans*: 71.

32. Pierre Belet and Anne Devailly, "Politiques familiales en Europe: le jeu des douze familles," *Espace social européen* (October 31, 1991): 22. For a review of the public responses to the problem of caring for infants and toddlers in Europe, see *Child Care, Parental Leave, and the Under 3s*, ed. Sheila B. Kamerman and Alfred J. Kahn (New York: Auburn Imprint of Greenwood Publishing Group, 1991).

33. This budget is part of a kit of planning materials collected by government authorities in the department of the Rhône for the benefit of those (whether local public authorities or nonprofit organizations) who might want to start a new child-care facility. See *Un mode d'accueil pour les enfants de 0 à 6 ans: guide pratique* (Lyon: Conseil Petite Enfance du Rhône, 1992).

34. Translated from Jaques Desigaux and Amédée Thévenet, *La garde des jeunes enfants* (Vendome: Presses Universitaires de France, 1980), 87.

35. French and American salaries cannot be compared in a straightforward way. In the United States, in 1993, employer and employee each paid social security taxes of 7.65 percent of the salary, for a total of 15.30 percent. Amounts that American employers pay for health insurance and into the unemployment insurance fund are excluded from salary. In France, the social security contribution is 45 percent of the salary, and includes the two latter charges. Of the 45 percent, the employee pays 13.45 percent. See *Barème social periodique*, 23/Nouvelle Série (Paris: Liaisons Sociales, 31 October 1993), 78. French social security payments go in part to pay for free or highly subsidized child care, and some housing assistance, which means that French salaries, particularly those earned by parents, go further than American salaries of the same nominal size. French workers get a month's paid vacation, considerably more than American workers.

36. This information is not, of course, given in the official and scholarly publications on which much of this chapter is based. However, it was alluded to in a scandalized tone by individuals in and out of government employ and is a situation that is despised by many people.

37. See *Le contrat enfance: une analyse des resultats au 31 decembre 1990* (Paris: Caisse Nationale des Allocations Familiales, 1991).

38. The National Academy of Sciences Panel on Child Care Policy concluded that there was a shortage of before-and-after-school care in the United States, where 2.1 million latchkey children were counted by the Census. See C. Hayes, J. Palmer, and M. Zaslow, *Who Cares for America's Children? Child Care Policy for the 1990s* (Washington: National Academy of Sciences Press, 1990): 232. A survey done in 1991 estimated that 1.7 million children, most in grade 3 or younger, were enrolled in before- and/or after-school programs, and that fees averaged $1.77 an hour. These programs serve a relatively small proportion of low-income families. See *National Study of Before & After School Programs, Executive Summary* (Washington: U.S. Department of Education, 1993).

39. "Les Haltes-Garderies, 1988," Observatoire des Équipments Sociaux (Paris: Caisse Nationale des Allocations Familiales, December 1990).

40. Norvez, *De la naissance à l'école*, 354.

41. Budget from *Un mode d'accueil pour les enfants de 0 à 6 ans: guide pratique* (Lyon: Conseil Petite Enfance du Rhône, 1992).

42. This information comes from the description of a *relais parentale* named "Passerelle" in Gennevilliers, contained in briefing material prepared by the Conseil Général des Hauts-de-Seine for a visiting group under the auspices of the French-American Foundation, January 13, 1994.

43. Caisse d'Allocations Familiales de Saône-et-Loire, "Les modes de garde des jeunes enfants" (Paris, n.d.).

44. OECD, *Child Care in OECD Countries*, 6.
45. See Commissariat Général Du Plan, "Inegalités et accueil de la petite enfance," (October 5, 1989). See, also, Frédérique Leprince, "La garde des jeunes enfants," *Données sociales 1987* (Paris: Institut National de la Statistique et des Études Économiques, 1987), 510–15.
46. *Carnet de santé maternité* (Lyon: Conseil Général du Rhône), 22–24.
47. *Barème social périodique*, 13/Nouvelle série (Paris: Liaisons Sociales, 30 April 1991), 34.
48. See *Barème social périodique* (Paris: Liaisons Sociales). These 1991 benefit levels (as well as those for French programs discussed in the rest of this chapter and the next) are given in issue No. 13, dated 30 April 1991. Those of 1995 are given in No. 30, 31 July 1995.
49. In 1990, American mothers using family day care reported spending $1.35 an hour, which would come to $234 per month for a child cared for forty hours per week. See Sandra L. Hofferth, April Brayfield, Sharon Deich, and Pamela Holcomb, *National Child Care Survey, 1990* (Washington: Urban Institute Press, 1991): 139.
50. Susan Pedersen, "Catholicism, Feminism, and the Politics of the Family during the Late Third Republic," in *Mothers of a New World: Maternalist Politics and the Origins of Welfare States*, ed. Seth Koven and Sonya Michel. (New York: Routledge, 1993).
51. "Qui va payer? Combien? Et Comment?" *CFDT-Magazine*, No. 157 (February 1991): 34.
52. U.S. Senate Committee on Labor and Human Resources, "Federal Job Training Programs: The Need for Overhaul," Hearings of 1–12 January 1995, statement of James J. Heckman, 260–72.

Chapter 4. French Payments to Raise Children's Living Standards

1. See *CAF statistiques; prestations familiales* (Paris: Caisse Nationale des Allocations Familiales, 1991) for a description of the programs that provide family benefits, and a chronology of their development. Periodic updates of benefit levels are found in the *Barème social périodique* series issued by Liaisons Sociales. In particular, benefit levels for 1991 are given in No. 13 dated 30 April 1991. Most of the material in this chapter comes from these two sources. See, also, Marie-Gabrielle David and Christophe Starzec, "France: A Diversity of Policy Options," in *Child Care, Parental Leave, and the Under 3s*, ed. Sheila B. Kamerman and Alfred J. Kahn (New York: Auburn Imprint of Greenwood Publishing Group, 1991).
2. The 1995 attempt to scale down deficits in the French social security system, met by massive strikes by public sector employees, involved a rise in payroll taxes and in the age of retirement.
3. *Contours et caractères; les femmes* (Paris: Institut National de la Statistique et des Études Économiques, 1991), 16–17.
4. New immigrants do not receive the *Revenue Minimum d'Insertion*. See this chapter.

5. In a footnote to his work on "family politics," Phillipe Madinier, one of France's leading experts on family benefits, said "Le système français des aides à la famille s'est progressivement diversifié et compliqué depuis une vingtaine d'années. Il atteint aujourd'hui un degrée de complexité probablement sans égal dans aucun pays." Or, "The French system of help to families has progressively changed and gotten more complicated in recent decades. It has attained a degree of complexity probably unequaled in any other country." See Centre d'Étude des Revenus et des Coûts, *Politique familiale et dimension de la famille* (Paris: La Documentation Française, 1992), 124. The cover of an issue of the bulletin of the organization that administers family benefits, the Caisse Nationale des Allocations Familiales, exhibits a cartoon of three puzzled bureaucrats, wheels spinning in their heads. The title of the bulletin is "Les prestations familiales: gerer la complexité" ("Family Benefits: Coping with the Complexity"). See *CAF Dossiers*, No. 3 (1987).

6. Benefit levels rise when children reach ten, and again when they reach fifteen.

7. Conseil Économique et Social, *La politique familiale française* (Paris: Direction des Journaux Officiels, 1991).

8. Ibid., 52.

9. Susan Pedersen, "Catholicism, Feminism, and the Politics of the Family during the Late Third Republic," in *Mothers of a New World: Maternalist Politics and the Origins of Welfare States*, ed. Seth Koven and Sonya Michel (New York: Routledge, 1993).

10. For a history of French family allowances after World War I, see Susan Pedersen, *Family, Dependence, and the Origins of the Welfare State: Britain and France, 1914–1945* (New York: Cambridge University Press, 1993).

11. The add-ons do not apply to the oldest child in a family of two children.

12. See Eurostat, *Digest of Statistics on Social Protection in Europe* (Luxembourg: European Communities Commission, 1993), 73. See, also, Jonathan Bradshaw, John Ditch, Hilary Holmes, and Peter Whiteford, *Support for Children: A Comparison of Arrangements in Fifteen Countries* (London: HMSO, 1993).

13. A family is not eligible to receive multiple payments under APJE or its extension in a given month, unless there have been multiple births.

14. The income earned in 1989 determined eligibility for this benefit in the first half of 1991. This probably has the effect of making more families eligible. See *Barème social periodique*, 23/Nouvelle Série (Paris: Liaisons Sociales, 31 October 1993), 53.

15. See *CAF statistiques: prestations familiales, 1991*, 70.

16. See Irwin Garfinkel, *Assuring Child Support: An Extension of Social Security* (New York: Russell Sage Foundation, 1992).

17. *CAF Statistiques: prestations familiales, 1991*, 247–50. The number of single parents refers to the year 1989, and is given in *Contours et caractères; les femmes*, 40.

18. Compare tables 4.1 and 6.1. Sources for housing expenditure data are given in the footnotes of these tables.

19. The benefit formula is given in terms of number of dependents rather than number of children. Thus, maintaining an aged parent in the household would count the same as maintaining an additional child. However, the parent's taxable income, such as an old-age benefit, would be counted in the household's income, and would in many cases push the family beyond the limits of eligibility.

20. Data on the precise proportion of funds under the APL program that go to families with children do not appear to be available. However, in 1990, 66.2 percent of the single persons or couples who were beneficiaries of the program had others in their household. Most of these others must have been children, since aged family members are endowed with pensions that would have put most households above the income ceiling for benefits. See *CAF statistiques; prestations de logement: premiers resultats 91* (Paris: Caisse Nationale des Allocations Familiales, 1991), 141, for distribution of beneficiaries by household composition.

21. *L'Allocation de Logement Social* was started in 1971, and is aimed at the elderly, the handicapped, young workers under twenty-five, the long-term unemployed, and those who have been absent from the job market and are in a program that helps them to reenter. Few of the beneficiaries of the ALS have children; 89 percent of them are in one-person households. See Nicole Tabard and Jean Olivier, "À chaque aide au logement sa localisation," *Recherches et prévisions* 29–30 (September–December 1992).

22. Certain government cash payments, such as the allowance for a new infant, are disregarded in calculating the family's benefit under this program.

23. It is possible to receive payments for more than one twelve-month period.

24. *La société française; données sociales 1993* (Paris: Institut National de la Statistique et des Études Économiques, 1993), 571.

25. See *CAF Statistiques; prestations familiales, 1991* (Paris: Caisse Nationale des Allocations Familiales, n.d.) 187, and V. Poubelle and B. Simonin, "Le RMI: un million d'allocataires en trois ans," in *La société française; données sociales 1993*, 550.

26. *Barème social periodique*, 13/Nouvelle Série (Paris: Liaisons Sociales, 30 April 1991), 73.

27. Poubelle and Simonin, "Le RMI."

28. Ibid.

29. Ibid.

30. See Christian Calzada and Pierre Volovich, "Protection sociale: le tournant des années quatre-vingt," in *La société française; données sociales 1993*, 516–23.

31. Jean-Marc Lhuillier, *Guide de l'aide sociale à l'enfance: droit et pratiques* (Paris: Berger Levrault, 1992).

32. Bénédicte Boisguérin, "L'aide sociale en 1986," *Données sociales 1990* (Paris: Institut National de la Statistique et des Études

Économiques, 1990), 419–22. See also *CAF statistiques; action sociale*, [19]86–91 (Paris: Caisse Nationale des Allocations Familiales).

33. "Notice pour remplir votre déclaration des revenus de 1990," booklet published by Imprimerie Nationale (November 1990).

34. Centre d'Étude des Revenus et des Coûts, *Politique familiale et dimension de la famille* (Paris: La Documentation Française, 1992), 39.

35. Estimate for 1990 from C. Eugene Steuerle and Jason Juffras, "A $1,000 Tax Credit for Every Child: A Base of Reform for the Nation's Tax, Welfare, and Health Systems," unpublished paper, The Urban Institute (April 1991), 16a.

36. For source of U.S. data on spending, refer to tables in chapter 6. For poverty reduction, see table 1.1.

37. Table 2.1 includes the Earned Income Tax Credit as a payment to improve living standards, rather than as a tax reduction. See discussion in chapter 6.

Chapter 5. Medical Services for Child Well-Being in France

1. See *OECD in Figures*, 1993 edition (Paris: Organisation for Economic Cooperation and Development, 1993): 44–45.

2. In France, as in many other countries, the control of medical costs is very difficult. At the current writing, the proportion of French physicians willing to agree to the official schedule of fees is falling. What patients pay over the officially allowed fee is not reimbursed.

3. Alisa Klaus's book, *Every Child a Lion: The Origins of Maternal and Infant Policy in the United States and France, 1890–1920* (Ithaca, N.Y.: Cornell University Press, 1993), was a source of material for this section.

4. Alain Norvez, *De la naissance à l'école* (Évry: Institut National d'Études Démographiques et Presses Universitaires de France, 1990). The records left by that program suggest that in some of the large cities as many as 40 percent of the babies were put out to wet-nurses.

5. See Klaus, *Every Child a Lion*.

6. Ibid. See, also, Karen Buhler-Wilkerson, *False Dawn: The Rise and Decline of Public Health Nursing, 1900–1930* (New York: Garland Publishing, Inc., 1989).

7. For a rather inconclusive discussion of this issue, see M. Manciaux, C. Jestin, M. Fritz, and D. Bertrand, "Child Health Care Policy and Delivery in France," *Pediatrics*, Supplement 1037–43 (1990).

8. G. Desplanques and M. Isnard, "La fécondité des étrangères diminue," in *La société française; données sociales 1993.* (Paris: Institut National de la Statistique et des Études Économiques, 1993), 46–53.

9. Recently, the responsibility for operating the PMI has been decentralized to the departments. However, the central government sets minimum standards for these operations.

10. Gail Richardson, *A Welcome for Every Child: How France Protects Maternal and Child Health—A New Frame of Reference for the United States* (Arlington, Va.: National Center for Education in Maternal and Child Health, 1994).

11. Norvez, *De la naissance à l'école*, 85.

12. Conseil Général du Rhône, "Le service de la protection maternelle et infantile et des vaccinations," January 13, 1993.

13. *Premiers éléments statistiques: PMI 1992* (Lyon: Conseil Général du Rhône, 1993).

14. Abortions, which are legal in France and are provided by the PMI, would presumably be reduced by better contraceptive use and better services for those who wish to keep their babies.

15. See chapter 2, for a discussion of conversion rates.

16. Pierre Buekens, Milton Kotelchuck, Béatrice Blondel, Finn Kristensen, Jian-Hua Chen, and Godelieve Masuy-Stroobant, "A Comparison of Prenatal Care Use in the United States and Europe," *American Journal of Public Health* 83 (1993): 31–36.

17. Monique Merrant-Dray, "Une prévention à domicile," in *Informations Sociales: P.M.I. Actualité* (Paris: Caisse Nationale des Allocations Familiales, October 1991), 49–52.

18. The prenatal home visits are usually weekly, but schedules of three times a week are not unusual, and they may be made even more often. The *sages-femmes* who make these visits are a highly selected group with four years of medical training. While their specialty is obstetrics-gynecology, they also have a good general medical background.

    A PMI brochure intended to introduce the idea of home visits to women who will receive them has on its cover an obviously pregnant, obviously middle-class Frenchwoman in smiling conversation with a stylishly dressed *sage-femme*. (Conseil Général, Seine Saint-Denis, "Accompagner les futures mamans: vos sages-femmes de PMI," n.d.) The two of them have finished the medical part of the visit and are enjoying a chat. The brochure explains that the aim of the *sage-femme* is to

    > accompany the mother and the infant throughout the months when life takes form and put their skill at the service of the future mom. . . . Regular visits to the home permit the *sage-femme* better to understand her, and to go over with her anything that could disturb the smooth progress of the pregnancy. A relationship of confidence is created. Sustained attention prevents many kinds of errors and problems.

    The brochure emphasizes that the visits are not compulsory, and that anyone is free to refuse them. In fact, however, very few women do.

19. Merrant-Dray, "Une prévention à domicile," 49.

20. Béatrice Blondel, Gérard Bréart, Joséfa Llado, and Michel Chartier, "Evaluation of the Home-Visiting System for Women with Threatened Preterm Labor: Results of a Randomized Controlled Trial,"

European Journal of Obstetrics and Gynecology and Reproductive Biology 34 (1990): 47–58.

21. *Carnet de santé maternité* (Lyon: Conseil Général du Rhône, n.d.).
22. This section makes extensive use of material in Colette de Saint-Sauveur, *Protection de la maternité et de l'enfance* (Paris: Masson, 1985).
23. In the Rhône branch of the PMI, which reports on its visits by age of the child, 50 percent of the babies younger than one year old receive visits. Some older children are also followed or visited occasionally: about 14 percent of the babies between two and three, and about 19 percent of children between three and four receive visits. See *Premiers éléments statistiques: PMI 1992* (Lyon: Conseil Général du Rhône, 1993).
24. De Saint-Sauveur, *Protection de la maternité*, 30–31.
25. Ibid.
26. Ministère des Affaires Sociales et de l'Integration, "Principaux indicateurs issus des certificats de santé," 1989.
27. De Saint-Sauveur, *Protection de la maternité*, 81.
28. See *Enfance et violences*, ed. Michel Andrieux and Jacqueline Rubellin-Devichi (Lyon: Presses Universitaires de Lyon, 1992).
29. Klaus, *Every Child a Lion*.
30. See Buekens, et al., "A Comparison of Prenatal Care Use."
31. Figures refer to 1991, and are from the Centers for Disease Control, reported in Kaiser Permanente, *Planning for Health* (August 1993): 3.
32. Robert Pear, "U.S. to Guarantee Free Immunization for Poor Children," *New York Times*, 16 August 1993, pp. 1, 15.
33. Robert Pear, "Audit by Congress Faults a Program for Free Vaccines," *New York Times*, 25 June 1995, p. 1.
34. Samuel J. Meisels and Sally Provence, *Screening and Assessment: Guidelines for Identifying Young Disabled and Developmentally Vulnerable Children and Their Families* (Arlington, Va.: Zero to Three National Center for Clinical Infant Programs, 1989).

PART III: AMERICAN PROGRAMS FOR CHILDREN, PAST AND FUTURE

Chapter 6. American Programs for Children: Keeping Millions Deprived

1. Figures on numbers in each group estimated from income distribution data in U.S. Bureau of the Census, *Statistical Abstract of the United States, 1993* (Washington, 1993), 464.
2. The median earnings for black female high-school graduates in 1951 was $12,182, about half of that for white male high-school graduates,

whose median was $23,710. For data on earnings by race, sex, and education, see U.S. Bureau of the Census, *Money Income of House-holds, Families, and Persons in the United States: 1991*, Current Population Reports, Series P-60, No. 180 (Washington: U.S. Government Printing Office, 1992), Table 29.

3.   D. Frum, "Righter Than Newt," *The Atlantic Monthly* (March 1995): 83–84.

4.   Senator Gramm is technically wrong in saying that mothers on welfare get "more money" than mothers working in a minimum-wage job for ten hours a day, even counting food stamps as "money." Nevertheless, given the in-kind benefits of child care and health care that the former get, the unfairness he observes is there.

5.   The official poverty line is not adjusted for such things as temperature differences, which make home heating costs differ. So Alaska's seemingly more generous benefits may fall below a reasonably drawn poverty line.

6.   Some states allow benefits to vary at the option of local governments, with the localities sharing some of the costs.

7.   The material in this section on the structure of benefit programs is taken from U.S. House of Representatives, Committee on Ways and Means, *1994 Greenbook: Overview of Entitlement Programs*, WMCP, 324–454 (Washington: U.S. Government Printing Office, 1994).

8.   Spalter-Roth's and Hartmann's estimates suggest that 20 percent of women receiving AFDC in the course of a two-year period received pay for work and AFDC checks simultaneously for at least four months of the period. Another 20 percent cycled on and off AFDC. See Roberta Spalter-Roth and Heidi Hartmann, "AFDC Recipients as Care-givers and Workers: A Feminist Approach to Income Security Policy for American Women," *Social Politics* 1 (Summer 1994): 190–210.

9.   For information on AFDC expenditures and recipients, see Vee Burke, "Cash and Noncash Benefits for Persons with Limited Income: Eligibility Rules, Recipient and Expenditure Data, FY 1990–92," 93-382 EPW (Washington: Congressional Research Service, 1993), and *1994 Greenbook*, 410.

10. *1994 Greenbook*, 755, 782.

11. See Ann Shola Orloff, "The Political Origins of America's Belated Welfare State," in *The Politics of Social Policy in the United States*, ed. Margaret Weir, Ann Shola Orloff, and Theda Skocpol (Princeton, N.J.: Princeton University Press, 1988).

12. See Charles Murray, *Losing Ground: American Social Policy, 1950–1980* (New York: Basic Books, 1984); and Mickey Kaus, *The End of Equality* (New York: Basic Books, 1992).

13. *1994 Greenbook*, 755, 782.

14. U.S. Bureau of Labor Statistics (BLS), *Consumer Expenditures in 1991*, BLS Report 835 (Washington, December 1992).

15. Originally, the EITC was restricted to families with children. Under the revisions of 1993, low-wage childless workers between twenty-five and sixty-four would qualify for a small credit.

16. The Republican majority in Congress has considered reduction in the EITC. Thus, it is by no means sure that the increases enacted in 1993 and scheduled to continue through 1996 will be permitted to occur. Republicans are calling attention to the high rate of fraudulent claims as a good reason to curtail the program.

17. For material on the provisions of the EITC and its history, see the *1994 Greenbook*, 699–704, from which the description here is derived.

18. Incomes at which the benefits change were also indexed. See Paul Leonard and Robert Greenstein, "The New Budget Reconciliation Law: Progressive Deficit Reduction and Critical Social Investments," Occasional Paper (Washington: Center on Budget and Policy Priorities, n.d.).

19. John Karl Scholtz, "The Earned Income Tax Credit: Participation, Compliance, and Antipoverty Effectiveness," *National Tax Journal*, March 1994, 63–87.

20. Ibid.

21. See Jonathan Bradshaw, John Ditch, Hilary Holmes, and Peter Whiteford, *Support for Children: A Comparison of Arrangements in Fifteen Countries* (London: HMSO, 1993), chapter 4.

22. See sources in table 6.1.

23. A small share of units may be rented to those with incomes up to 80 percent of the median.

24. Vee Burke, "Cash and Noncash Benefits for Persons With Limited Income: Eligibility Rules, Recipient and Expenditure Data, FY 1990–92," 93-382 EPW (Washington: Congressional Research Service, 1993), 113.

25. Department of Housing and Urban Development (HUD), *Characteristics of HUD-Assisted Renters and Their Units in 1989* (Washington, March 1992), 78, 120.

26. Ibid.

27. Ibid., 27.

28. See the *1994 Greenbook*, 783–813. Two other groups get benefits under Medicaid: the low-income disabled and the "medically needy." Retired citizens covered by social security get medical benefits under Medicare, which is an entirely separate program. Medicare does not provide for unlimited nursing-home care. Old people needing long-term care in a nursing home who exhaust other benefits and their assets may qualify for Medicaid, which will pay for their care.

29. *1994 Greenbook*, 811.

30. *Statistical Abstract of the United States, 1993*, 115.

31. See U.S. Bureau of the Census, *Child Support and Alimony: 1983*, Current Population Reports, Special Studies Series P-23, (Supplemental Report), No. 148 (Washington: Government Printing Office, 1986).

32. See Irwin Garfinkel, *Assuring Child Support: An Extension of Social Security* (New York: Russell Sage Foundation, 1992).

33. See source notes in table 6.1.

34. School programs in grades one and above also serve a custodial function, although this is not commonly acknowledged.

35. Evelyn Weber, *The Kindergarten: Its Encounter with Educational Thought in America* (New York: Teachers College, 1971).

36. Doris P. Fromberg, *The Full Day Kindergarten* (New York: Teachers College, 1987).

37. National Center for Education Statistics, *Digest of Educational Statistics, 1993* (Washington, 1993) 62. One may conjecture that a higher proportion of the private kindergartens offer full-day operation than the public ones. For public kindergartens, about 35 percent are full time.

38. R. H. McKey, A. N. Smith, and S. S. Aitken, *The Impact of Head Start on Children, Families, and Communities: Final Report of the Head Start Evaluation, Synthesis, and Utilization Project* (Washington: U.S. Department of Health and Human Services, 1985).

39. "Project Head Start Statistical Fact Sheet" (Washington: Administration on Children, Youth, and Families, Department of Health and Human Services, January 1994).

40. See *Head Start Program Performance Standards* (Washington: Administration on Children, Youth, and Families, Department of Health and Human Services, 1993). For training of teachers, see Gwen Morgan, *Making a Career of It* (Boston: Wheelock College, 1993).

41. "Project Head Start Statistical Fact Sheet."

42. See Abbie Gordon Klein, *The Debate over Child Care, 1969–1990; A Sociohistorical Analysis* (Albany, N.Y.: State University of New York Press, 1992), from which much of the material in this section is derived.

43. U.S. General Accounting Office, *Early Childhood Programs: Multiple Programs and Overlapping Target Groups*, GAO/HEHS-95-4FS (Washington, 1994).

44. See *Cost, Quality, and Child Outcomes in Child Care Centers, Technical Report*, ed. Suzanne W. Helburn (Denver: Department of Economics, University of Colorado, 1995).

45. *1994 Greenbook*, 543.

46. *Who Cares for America's Children? Child Care Policy for the 1990's*, ed. Cheryl D. Hayes, John L. Palmer, and Martha J. Zaslow (Washington: National Academy Press, 1990), 135.

47. "Cost, Quality, and Child Outcomes in Child Care Centers," Executive Summary, ed. Suzanne W. Helburn (Denver: Department of Economics, University of Colorado, 1995).

48. Ibid., 11.

49. For a more extended treatment of the history of child-care legislation, see Sandra L. Hofferth, "The 101st Congress: An Emerging Agenda for Children in Poverty," in *Child Poverty and Public Policy*, ed. Judith A. Chafel (Washington: Urban Institute Press, 1993).

50. Estimate by the author based on material in Vee Burke, "Cash and Noncash Benefits for Persons with Limited Income."

51. Ibid.

Chapter 7. Reducing Child Poverty by Helping Working Parents

1. Of women holding jobs in 1992, nineteen out of a thousand had given birth to a baby the previous year. The comparable figure for women who were not in the labor force was thirty-five out of a thousand. (See *Statistical Abstract of the United States, 1993*, 79, 81.) However, not all of the difference in birth expectations or births between women in jobs and women out of jobs is caused by the difference in labor force status. Causation also runs the other way. Also, certain groups may traditionally exhibit low labor force participation for women and a high birthrate, while other groups may exhibit the opposite pattern.

2. An extensive discussion of the problems with the official methodology is provided by Patricia Ruggles, *Drawing the Line: Alternative Poverty Measures and Their Implications for Public Policy* (Washington: Urban Institute Press, 1990). See, also, Isabel Sawhill, "Poverty in the U.S.: Why Is It So Persistent?" *Journal of Economic Literature* 26 (1988): 1073–119.

3. The poverty line was initially intended to represent an after-tax requirement. In practice, the Census Bureau classifies a family as poor or nonpoor on the basis of its reported before-tax income.

4. See Trudi J. Renwick and Barbara R. Bergmann, "A Budget-Based Definition of Poverty, with an Application to Single-Parent Families," *Journal of Human Resources* 28 (Winter 1993): 1–24. Adequacy standards for each commodity group are derived almost entirely from U.S. government-set standards and are allowed to vary where appropriate depending on the labor force status of the parent, the ages of the children, the area and region of residence, and the availability to the family of noncash benefits from the government, an employer, or a relative. Family size adjustments are made separately for each commodity group.

5. See *Measuring Poverty: A New Approach*, ed. Constance F. Citro and Robert T. Michael (Washington: National Academy Press, 1995).

6. Median weekly earnings of full-time year-round workers are given in U.S. Bureau of the Census, *Statistical Abstract of the United States, 1994* (Washington, 1994), 429.

7. See Robert Haveman, "The Help for Working Parents Plan: Some Potentials and Problems," *Feminist Economics* 1 (Summer 1995): 105–108. See also his book *Starting Even: An Equal Opportunity Program to Combat the Nation's New Poverty* (New York: Simon and Schuster, 1988) which calls for subsidies to increase employers' demand for unskilled labor and the establishment of "capital accounts" that workers can draw on for the cost of skill training. He also advocates refundable tax credits, which would be the equivalent of cash grants to all residents. The only special program for families with children he suggests is an improved child support enforcement system through the tax system.

8. See *1994 Greenbook*, 335.

9. See Robert E. Goodin, *Reasons for Welfare: The Political Theory of the Welfare State* (Princeton, N.J.: Princeton University Press, 1988).

10. See the discussion of the recommendations of the National Commission on Children in chapter 8, particularly conservatives' attitudes toward out-of-home child care.

11. The EITC was scheduled to rise above this level in 1996. See chapter 6.

12. For the family with an adult earning a minimum wage under the HWP proposal, the EITC and food stamps would cost $3,411 combined, child care would cost $9,600, and medical insurance $3,749, for a total of $16,760. Subtracting taxes of $851 leaves a cost to the public of $15,909. The "full welfare" solution would cost $10,847 in AFDC and food stamps plus $3,749 for Medicaid, for a total of $14,596.

13. In an average state in 1993, for the family on AFDC, the AFDC benefits and food stamps cost $4,404 and $2,690, respectively, plus $3,749 for Medicaid, for a total of $10,843.

14. This net additional cost to taxpayers does not include the cost of whatever food stamp and EITC benefits the family is already getting.

15. See Barbara R. Bergmann and Sherry Wetchler, "Child Support Awards: State Guidelines Versus Public Opinion," *Family Law Quarterly* 29 (Fall 1995): 483–93.

16. Irwin Garfinkel, *Assuring Child Support: An Extension of Social Security* (New York: Russell Sage Foundation, 1992).

17. In 1991, of the seventy million people not covered by government-provided or employer-provided health insurance, thirty-six million people, or slightly over half, had health insurance, presumably self-purchased. See *Statistical Abstract of the United States, 1993*, 115.

18. Agnar Sandmo, "Ex-post-welfare Economics and the Theory of Merit Goods," *Economica* 50 (February 1983): 19–33.

19. Sandra Hofferth, April Brayfield, Sharon Deich, and Pamela Holcomb *National Child Care Survey, 1990* (Washington: Urban Institute, 1991), 178.

20. Helburn, ed., "Cost, Quality, and Child Outcomes in Child Care Centers."

21. The figure on single mothers in poverty is from the *Statistical Abstract of the United States, 1994*, 479. The estimate of their labor force participation is from Roberta Spalter-Roth and Heidi Hartmann, "AFDC Recipients as Care-givers and Workers," *Social Politics* 1 (Summer 1994): 190–210.

22. *Employment and Earnings*, January 1993.

23. This estimate is based on the assumption that the 40 percent of this group that worked part of the year had jobs for two-tenths of a year, on average, and that those entering the labor force included all those who experienced part-year employment. The derivation of the number in the text is:

$$3.7 \times 0.6 \times (1{-}0.4 \times 0.2) = 2.0$$

24. *Statistical Abstract of the United States, 1993*, 378, table 597.

25. Robert Haveman, "The Help for Working Parents Plan: Some Potentials and Problems," *Feminist Economics* 1 (Summer 1995): 106.

26. These programs cost the federal government $24.8 billion in 1994. For an assessment of their effectiveness, see U.S. Senate Committee on Labor and Human Resources, *Federal Job Training Programs: The Need for Overhaul*, Hearings of 1–12 January 1995, statement of James J. Heckman, 260–72.

27. See Sandra K. Danziger and Sheldon Danziger, "Will Welfare Recipients Find Work?" in *Welfare Reform: An Analysis of the Issues*, ed. Isabel V. Sawhill (Washington: Urban Institute, 1995). The authors, reporting on a study by Sandra K. Danziger and Sherrie A. Kossoudji, assume that the general assistance clients would be more able than welfare clients to find and keep jobs, a point of view opposite to the one I take here.

28. Spalter-Roth and Hartmann, "AFDC Recipients as Care-givers and Workers," 198.

29. Jean Kimmel, "Child Care Costs as a Barrier to Employment for Single and Married Mothers," unpublished paper (Kalamazoo, Mich.: W.E. Upjohn Institute for Employment Research, October 1994).

30. Gregory Acs, "Do Welfare Benefits Promote Out-of-Wedlock Childbearing?" in *Welfare Reform; An Analysis of the Issues* (Washington: Urban Institute, 1995). See, also, David T. Ellwood, *Poor Support: Poverty in the American Family* (New York: Basic Books, 1988). Even if the availability of AFDC benefits does not increase births, it may enable and therefore encourage poor teenage mothers to leave their parents' household and set up households of their own.

Chapter 8. Can We Conquer Child Poverty in America Through Political Action?

1. National Commission on Children, *Beyond Rhetoric: A New American Agenda for Children and Families* (Washington: National Commission on Children, 1991), viii.

2. Ibid., xviii. However, one of the Republican Commissioners took pains to argue in a letter appended to the report that "most of America's children are doing well, and it is somewhat unfair to blame America for the erroneous choice of behavior of some individuals. America is not to be blamed for the drug babies, teen mothers, or one parent families . . ." (497).

3. Employers with twenty-five or more employees would be required to provide coverage immediately; employers with fewer than twenty-five would be required to provide coverage at the end of five years.

4. According to the commission's forecasts, states and localities would realize an estimated $2.5 billion in savings on the cost of health care

for people who would be covered by federal or private insurance under the plan, and employers who currently provide insurance would also save, as cost-shifting diminishes. The commission's ideas for covering children's health needs were remarkably similar to the ones subsequently embodied in President Clinton's defeated proposals for universal health coverage. Nine of the eleven Republican-appointed members of the commission objected strongly to the employer mandates as costing jobs and argued that "new taxes and more government interference with the market will, we believe, lead us not to better health care for all, but to skyrocketing health costs, and health care of poorer quality" (167). They argued that the already enacted phased-in extension of Medicaid to cover all poor children would eventually take care of the most urgent part of the problem.

5. Ibid., 273.

6. Ibid., 90.

7. Ibid., 493.

8. However, the commission apparently could not agree on whether to support funding for one year of service per eligible child, entailing an addition of $0.8 billion to the budget, or to support funding for two years, which would have entailed an addition of $2.4 billion.

9. The NCC viewed the child tax credit as something that would be added to existing welfare benefits, which would be left undisturbed (see table 5.5 on p. 111 of the report). However, if the credit were ever to be enacted, it is not clear that states could be kept from lowering AFDC payments in response.

10. Children's Defense Fund, *Vanishing Dreams: The Economic Plight of America's Young Families* (Washington, 1992), 3.

11. Children's Defense Fund, *Child Poverty in America* (Washington, 1991) 29–33; id., *Vanishing Dreams*, 26–31.

12. In the CDF's 1994 list of policy proposals, the replacement of the personal exemption for children with the refundable tax credit is placed eighth on the list, while the creation of more job opportunities, including public sector jobs targeted for the poor, is put first. See Arloc Sherman, *Wasting America's Future: The Children's Defense Fund Report on the Costs of Child Poverty* (Boston: Beacon Press, 1994), xxvii.

13. The CDF's major 1994 publication devotes only one of its 183 pages to its recommended policy agenda. Government-sponsored child care (in unspecified amounts) appears there among its major agenda items. The document does contain a novelty for CDF—a short discussion of what it would take to end child poverty. It speaks of a "blend of strategies [that would] not only end child poverty, but ... also would improve incentives and opportunities for lower-income parents to work and form stable families" (117). The set of strategies is not spelled out in any detail, but might include "giving jobless parents part-time jobs and providing child care, wage supplements, and direct cash assistance" (117). A cost estimate of $62 billion a year is

given. To indicate the tentativeness of the exercise, however, CDF cautions that this is merely an example, and that "[i]t is *not* CDF's recommended strategy" (117, emphasis in original). See Sherman, *Wasting America's Future*, 116–19.

14. Thus, a person getting $5 an hour from an employer would get a subsidy that would bring the reward to $6.50. See Haveman, "The Help for Working Parents Plan." See, also, Robert Haveman, *Starting Even: New Policies for the Nation's New Poverty* (New York: Simon and Schuster, 1988).

15. *Statistical Abstract of the United States, 1994*, 55, 80.

16. Charles Murray, *Losing Ground: American Social Policy, 1950–1980* (New York: Basic Books, 1984).

17. Some of the latter have suggested that the orphanages would be supported by private donations, and would therefore cost the taxpayers little or nothing.

18. Penelope Leach, *Children First* (New York: Alfred A. Knopf, 1994).

19. See *Statistical Abstract of the United States, 1994*, page 402.

20. See the remarks of Jerry Regier, quoted above in this chapter.

21. See discussion and references in chapter 6.

22. This section takes material from the author's "Child Care: The Key to Ending Child Poverty," in *Social Policies For Children*, ed. Irwin Garfinkel, Jennifer L. Hochschild, and Sara S. McLanahan (Washington: Brookings Institution, 1995).

23. See table 1.1.

✣ INDEX ✣

Boldface numbers refer to tables and figures.